Do Pirates

Wear Pajamas?

Other books by Gordon Dalbey

Healing the Masculine Soul

Sons of the Father:

Healing the Father-Wound in Men Today

Fight like a Man:

A New Manhood for a New Warfare

No Small Snakes:

A Journey into Spiritual Warfare

Broken by Religion, Healed by God:

Restoring the Evangelical, Sacramental,

Pentecostal, Social Justice Church

Religion vs. Reality

Facing the Home Front in Spiritual Warfare

Pure Sex

The Spirituality of Desire

Loving to Fight or Fighting to Love

Winning the Spiritual Battle for Your Marriage

Gordon Dalbey may be contacted
for speaking engagements and other resources at
Box 61042, Santa Barbara, CA 93160
www.abbafather.com

Do Pirates Wear Pajamas?

and Other Mysteries in
the Adventure of Fathering

by

Gordon Dalbey

CivitasPress

Publishing inspiring and redemptive ideas.[sm]

Gordon Dalbey
Copyright © 2013 by Gordon Dalbey
All rights reserved
ISBN # 978-0615817453
Published by Civitas Press, LLC
San Jose, CA,
www.civitaspress.com

Cover sketch by Netta Jones nettajones1@verizon.net
Printed in the United States of America

> **"Dad, I want to give my son the best."**
> *Gordon Dalbey, 1944 -*
>
> **"No, you want him to *have* the best."**
> *Earle Dalbey, 1916 - 2010*

Contents

"It's not an adventure
unless it's a little scary."

Never trust a dad
without spit-up on his pajamas.

Whatever you don't forgive your father for,
you'll do to your son.

The first half of life we want to be like adults;
the second half, to be like children.

Like Jesus, the ministry of the child
is to restore innocence to this world.

A boy will heed his father's No only
as deeply as he has enjoyed his father's Yes.

In order to grow into his destiny,
a boy must root in his heritage.

Nothing helps you know God's love
like having a child of your own.

If you obey just for your father's approval,
you can disobey when you can discredit him.

Watch for what God is doing in your child
and bless it.

Father God sets boundaries not to deny us pleasure,
but to protect us from pain.

A father with a daughter
must teach her how men think.

The joy of fathering
is the fountainhead of its tasks.

A father imparts courage and strength by
standing with his son in fear and weakness.

The lessons of fathering
are the character of God

When Saul saw David going out to fight Goliath,
he asked Abner, the commander of his army,
"Abner, whose son is he?"
"I have no idea, Your Majesty," Abner answered.
"Then go and find out," Saul ordered.
(1 Samuel 17:55)

Foreword

MANY YEARS AGO, in a land far, too far away, my three-year-old son sat excitedly on my lap before bedtime while together we read a picture book based on *Treasure Island*. As Long John Silver, cutlass in hand, chased young Jim across the page and through the jungle, the boy within my arms suddenly knit his brow and looked up at me.

"Daddy," he burst out, "do pirates wear pajamas?"

Startled, I drew back. "Uh, well, that's…uh, a really great question!" I managed.

When I was a much younger man and unmarried, my father once told me, **"If you never have children, you'll miss out on one of life's greatest adventures."**

He was right.

But I hasten to add, it's no cakewalk. Adventures, by nature, often lead to unexpected places, where your comfortable assumptions can get picked off quicker than pieces-of-eight on a treasure chest.

As my son began growing, I wanted him to join me in some work to make him feel useful. When he reached five, I asked him to help me stuff envelopes with a flyer promoting my books.

Tentative but agreeable, he walked up to the coffee table where envelopes, flyers, and stamps lay waiting. "What's all this stuff for?" he asked.

I lifted a sheet from the stack. "These are flyers about the books I've written!" I noted cheerfully. "We'll fold them up and send them to people."

The boy raised an inquisitive eyebrow. "So," he asked matter-of-factly, "is this how you trick people into buying your books?"

"Actually," I offered lamely, "it's called 'advertising'."

You may have noticed by now that I didn't answer the question about pirates and their overnight attire. That's because I didn't have a clue how to. I still don't, if the truth be told.[1]

But that, of course, is what adventures are all about.

ADVENTURE MEANS SCARY

Once, when he was about six, my son and I went for a hike in the woods and found ourselves up against a sloping hill packed with boulders. We took a long and measured look, nodded finally, and up we went. Scraping knees and clinging onto whatever cracks and knobs we could, at last we stood triumphantly together at the peak.

"Whew!" I exclaimed in relief. "That was sure an adventure!" Pausing to whack boulder dust off my pants, I added "—but it was pretty scary."

"Daddy," the boy countered, brushing aside my disclaimer like so much boulder dust, "**it's not an adventure unless it's a little scary.**"

He, too, was right.

Welcome to the adventure of fathering. It is indeed more than a little scary.

"I'm sure when you first became a father," I often joke with men at my conferences, "you all got that bestseller, *How to be a Perfect Dad in 5 Easy Lessons*— right?"

The laughter that spreads widely around the room tells me I'm not alone.

"Me neither," I confess. "Actually, it went out of print long before my dad and I were born!"

My license to write a book about fathering is my experience with my son and only child. Nevertheless, I don't believe that the adventure of fathering is reserved for immediate blood relationships. A caring man—stepfather, grandfather, uncle, coach or mentor—can contribute significantly to a child's life. And so I've included two chapter stories about a fatherless boy whom I took under my wing some years before I became a dad myself. In addition, the Appendix has an article on how to change generational patterns of fathering and another on tips for single dads.

This book is for men, as only men can be fathers. Since only boys grow up to be men, the focus here is on sons. Nevertheless, I believe it can speak to men with daughters as well.

I listen to friends of mine with daughters and realize how that experience has its own challenges and joys, and can be significantly different from mine (see my chapter, "Fathers and Daughters" in *Healing the Masculine Soul*). Lacking that experience myself, still I would venture that the larger truth and lessons in my stories here might apply as well to you and your daughter.

Speaking of experience I lack, this would be a good place to salute the other half of the father equation. What a woman goes through in order to bear and bring forth a baby is a marvel to any man privileged to witness it. **But I would never presume to understand what childbirth and motherhood is really like for a woman.**

Mary gave me a clue when we went to a party a few weeks after our son was born. Holding the baby gingerly in my arms, I struggled to appear calm and in control. Eventually, an older man came over and reached out to shake my hand; awkwardly, I shifted the baby in order to reach back.

"Congratulations on being a dad!" the man smiled. "It can be tough at the beginning, but you'll manage OK." Turning to Mary, he added, "What great fun to become parents!"

Considering graciously these two cavalier dads, Mary—who, as you'll see in a later chapter, had suffered an excruciating labor— smiled thinly at me. "Yours was the easy part," she noted.

Stifling an urge to remind that I personally had not designed the gender-specific nature of childbirth, I nodded with due respect. As any man will tell you, conception is a truly delightful miracle. Childbirth, on the other hand, is…well, let's just say they don't call it "labor" for nothing.

FATHERS' LABOR

Having said that—all too briefly, granted—I would humbly suggest here that in fact, a special kind of labor is required of fathers as well.

A man wants to get in on the action with this tiny human being who bears his very image and name. This desire only gets stronger as he sees his wife go through the graphic physical demands of another life growing inside her: the nine-months' diet and activity adjustments, the pain of delivery, and challenges of nursing. Clearly, the overwhelming urgency of this experience creates an intense bond, both physical and emotional, between baby and Mom.

Dad, however, experiences none of those bodily demands—nor the bond they generate.

It's harder at first for the man to engage.

The mother-bond is organic. To be one with the mother is the natural condition of the flesh from its very genesis in the womb. Union with Dad, however, lacks that component of the flesh and therefore needs a more deliberate emotional and spiritual connection.

It's hard. From his relative distance, how does a dad relate to someone who spends his time crying, filling up his diapers, sleeping, and nursing your otherwise well-rested and responsive wife? I do believe, as we'll see in a later chapter, that God has given men a "father instinct." But clearly, the father-bond must grow out of something besides physical touch and bodily needs.

From the get-go, a dad is nine months behind the starting line. The father-bond is not as natural as a mother's experience. **Its essence, therefore, must be *super*-natural. As such, it requires a heart operation to recognize and engage.**

That's what this book is about.

In fact, God promises in the very last verses of the Hebrew Scriptures that He will send the prophet Elijah to make way for Jesus, in order that He might "turn the hearts of the fathers to their children and the hearts of the children to their fathers" (Malachi 4:5,6NIV). Significantly, He does not promise to turn the hearts of mothers to their children and the hearts of children to their mothers—likely because that's an organic given.

I'm glad He steps in like this to provide for us dads. In fact, the more He does it, the more confidence I get as a father. The more I surrender to Jesus, that is, the more Father God reveals His heart for me, and in turn, opens my heart to my son.

Sure, it's not all fun. Fathering exposes your weak spots, calls for sacrifice, a readiness to be wounded, and perseverance. Frustrating schedule changes, tense doctor visits, and eating out with more food on the floor than on the high chair—plus plenty of other upsets—come with the package.

Over the years, however, I came to see challenges like these as a father's labor pains—which have bonded me increasingly to my son. In fact, it's all taught me how God sees us—even His own sacrifice, readiness to be wounded, and persevering love (see Hosea 11).

Even as both pain and joy deepen your faith, the lessons of fathering are the character of God. The more you know God as your own true Father, the more you can receive from Him to give your own children.

In the world, that is, a man's identity is determined by the question, "What does he do?" In the Kingdom of God—as King Saul asks Abner in the opening Scripture--it's "Who's son is he?" [2]

Soon after my first book *Healing the Masculine Soul* promised in 1988 to pioneer a Christian men's movement, people began asking me, "When are you going to write a book on fathering?"

"Call me when I've got some experience!" I laughed.

On the occasion of my son's 21st birthday, having established himself away from home in college, it seemed appropriate to revisit that challenge while I grieve my loss and celebrate his victory.

These stories I've collected over the years shine brighter as I try to grasp what so many other dads told me 21 years ago: "Enjoy this time—it'll be over before you know it!"

They, too, were right. It's gone by in a flash.

But I took their advice and really did enjoy it.

May these stories help you do the same.

Introduction

Welcoming the Adventure

*Whoever welcomes in my name one such child
as this, welcomes me.* (Matthew 18:5)

"YOU KNOW, WE REALLY NEED to begin thinking about starting a family."

Amid the otherwise comforting aroma of scrambled eggs and salsa, Mary leaned ever so matter-of-factly into our breakfast table, shortly before our first anniversary—and waited.

Suddenly the newspaper I was scanning seemed to grab my attention. "Well, I guess...I mean, yeah, I think that's probably a good idea," I mumbled, fidgeting with the pages.

"So how do you feel about being a father?" Mary asked.

A woman cuts to the bottom line fast on this sort of thing.

"'Being a father'? Oh, excited...," I allowed, hesitating. "Feel" questions are not my favorite; nervously, I turned to the next page and stared vacantly at The Big Tire Sale.

Sighing at last, I laid down my paper and turned to Mary. "...but scared."

It was true. Neither of us had ever had children. Sure, at 46, I'd thought about it off and on over the years. But Mary's question was on target. We didn't have a lot of time left.

Still, we had a good life. Mary, a psychologist, was running a Christian counseling center. We loved each other, enjoyed our jobs and the freedom to come and go. We exercised regularly, ate healthy, and slept well—all night long, in fact.

"Your life will never be the same," everyone with children warned. But as we talked honestly that morning, we realized that was precisely the point. I didn't want my life to be the same. I'd already traveled the world, taught school, pastored churches, written a bestselling book, spoken on radio and TV shows.

Exciting as all this had been at the time, the prospect of a repeat cycle by itself now felt flat. As two independent "religious professionals," Mary and I tried to imagine what it would be like to be parents. Embarrassing as this is to recall, we wondered, How would we fit a child into our busy schedules?

THE BEST LIFE

At last, we decided to check the Bible for passages about children. What we read startled, humbled, and convicted us. **Children, we saw, are not a burden who obstruct "the good life," but a blessing from God who facilitate the best life**:

"May the Lord give you children," the Psalmist proclaimed, "you and you descendants! May you be blessed by the Lord, who made heaven and earth!" (Ps. 115:4,5). Again, "Children are a gift from the Lord; they are a real blessing" (Ps. 127:3).

And more: "Your wife will be like a fruitful vine within your house; your children will be like olive shoots around your table. Lo, thus shall the man be blessed who fears the Lord" (Ps. 128:3,4 RSV). Introducing his family to his brother Esau, Jacob declared, "These are the children whom God has been good enough to give me" (Gen. 33:5).

These timeless words not only turned our minds around, but brought us to our knees together at the foot of our bed. There, we confessed—as Jesus chided the first disciples—that we hadn't trusted His purposes and "welcomed" the child in His name.

We begged God's forgiveness for our near-sighted view of happiness and freedom, cast a spirit of "independence" from us both, and confessed anew our dependence on Him and each other. We surrendered and poured out our hearts, together telling God at last how much we longed for a child, and cried out the pain for years of not having one.

We realized that in our single years we had stopped hoping for children for fear of being disappointed. **We were so busy doing our own thing because we hadn't trusted God to do His thing.**

Though neither of us had ever had a child, we were old enough to know that God's thing is not always to make life easy for us.

"The Holy Spirit is like my children," as my seminary pastor Rev. Herb Davis once said years ago. "When we're taking a trip in the car, I set my watch and make sure all the kids go to the bathroom before we leave. A few minutes later, when we hit the freeway on schedule, I see that open road and click in my cruise control, lean back at last and relax.

"And just about then, I hear a small voice from the back seat: 'Daddy, I have to go!'"

CONTROLLED AGENDAS

As a dad myself now, I can say that a child truly is upsetting— especially when you cling for security to your own controlled agendas. The weak, needy, and vulnerable child reflects our true condition in this broken world—no matter how "adult" we may pretend to be—and thereby, mocks our pretensions of power and can unleash our deepest fears. That's why the disciples "scolded" parents for bringing their children to Jesus for His blessing: the disciples were using religion to appear mature and thereby, to cover the shame of their child-like inadequacy (Mark 10:13).

To summarize: **Never trust a dad without spit-up on his pajamas.**

Fathering means plenty of sacrifice and pain. But its rich lessons— and yes, unmatched joy—make it well worth it for any man willing to persevere in the adventure with an open heart. In fact, during my first few years as a dad, I found myself less surprised by the pain than by the joy—which often left me strangely angry.

My pre-dad life experience, that is, from Peace Corps to pastoring, had prepared me for the tough work of fathering: the smelly diapers, sleepless nights, pruned social life, Di-Gel dinners, and sex fasts. But I wasn't prepared for the joy.

Sure, you'll make your mistakes like all of us. But even more surely, the Father "from whom all fatherhood in heaven and on earth receives its true name" has a special heart of mercy for His sons who are fathers (Ephes. 3:14NIV footnote). Not only to forgive us, but to bless us far beyond what we deserve—even, especially, in the struggle.

That's called grace. As you cry out to Him and ask forgiveness from Him and from your children, He brings you back together—and restores your excitement for the adventure.

Imagine your little son sitting in your lap at breakfast as you squint in frustration at your newspaper spotted with oatmeal. Suddenly a small voice announces, "I like my daddy!" What can you do but worship the Living God—whose "unfailing love and mercy still continue, fresh as the morning, as sure as the sunrise" (Lam. 3:22-23)?

You know you've been redeemed. And when he bumps his head and cries, "Daddy, talk to Jesus!" you know why.

In my early days as a dad, I wondered, Why didn't anyone ever tell me about this overwhelming joy in being a father?

The answer, I eventually realized, is that we men have not learned to value the child.

True, my dad told me I'd miss out on one of life's greatest adventures if I never became a father myself. I'm grateful for that fatherly word.

But never in all my adult travels did any other older man tell me even that much about being a father—neither while studying at the very finest universities, attending churches of virtually every denomination, listening to politicians of every stripe, or reading the most esteemed authors. From cereal boxes and movies to commercials and sermons, various men told me that nothing in this world is more satisfying than winning a ball game, having sex with a woman, making money, succeeding professionally, reading the Bible, and serving the poor.

Each of those activities can be very good. But never in my life did an older man tell me the truth: No life experience makes you feel more in touch with God's very heart, more determined to battle for his Kingdom, and thereby, more genuinely like a man than being a father.

I was ripped off. As a man, I felt as if I'd been lied to, even cheated out of a supreme pleasure virtually my entire adult life.

Yet in my heart, I know the truth: The old men did not lie to me. They told me what they genuinely believed to be true, out of their own wounded boyhood.

There's great joy in the stories you'll read here. But that very joy causes me even now to grieve sometimes for what my forefathers missed.

It's natural to let your own painful experiences as a boy shape your later playbook as a dad yourself. Often, however, those childhood wounds can short-circuit the joy available to you as a dad today with your own family (see my book *Sons of the Father: Healing the Father-Wound in Men*).

And yet...

Living with someone thrilled by wiggly worms on a wet sidewalk, who shouts, "Daddy, let's wrestle and roar like lions," who races laughing into your arms when you come home, who cries, "Daddy, pray to Jesus!" when he bumps his head—for a man, that's called a second chance. Not just for you, but for the men of your heritage.

Don't miss it.

1

Can Daddy Come out and Play?
The Ministry of the Child

> *At that time the disciples came to Jesus asking,*
> *"Who is the greatest in the Kingdom of heaven?"*
>
> *So Jesus called a child, had him stand in front of*
> *them, and said, "I assure you, that unless you change*
> *and become like children, you will never enter the*
> *Kingdom of heaven. The greatest in the Kingdom of*
> *heaven is the one who humbles himself and becomes*
> *like this child."* (Matt. 18:1-3)

IN THE ROBIN WILLIAMS MOVIE *HOOK*, workaholic businessman Peter has forgotten that he's in fact Peter Pan, and thereby, has forsaken his child-like heart. In a striking scene, he and his pre-teen son are seated together in an airplane. Out of boredom, the boy takes out his baseball mitt and begins to toss a ball up in the air from his seat.

"Would you stop acting like a child!" the father explodes.

"But Dad," the boy protests, "I AM a child."

The rest of this rejuvenating film focuses on restoring the child—and thereby, destiny and power—in a man emasculated by his adult ambitions.

"We spend the first half of our lives trying to become like adults," as someone older and wiser once noted, "and the last half trying to become like children again."

It's sad, but true. Striving to "grow up and be responsible" at best makes us forget what it feels like to be a child; at worst, it makes us scorn the child—who of course, is too much like us: weak, needy, and powerless. What we disallow in ourselves, we often scorn similarly and even punish in others.

Once, the disciples asked Jesus, "Who is the greatest in the Kingdom of heaven?" As His "answer," He presented them not with a sports hero, film star, President, or even megachurch pastor, but rather, with a child.

What? we can imagine the disciples' thinking. *Has Jesus gone mad?*

Or indeed, has this world gone mad, seduced by and drunk on worldly powers that promise falsely to cover our inadequacy?

Why, oh why, does it take so long for us to see as Jesus sees?

Maybe because we, too, are His disciples.

As we "grow up," that is, we respond to the demands of the world for jobs, money, control, esteem. And then one terrifying day, you wake up and realize you haven't welcomed the child in your heart; in fact, you've scorned and driven him away. The wonder, the hope, the passion, the fun—and the humility which invites them—where did they go? In spite of your best efforts to appear "mature," you find yourself yearning for more freedom, more fun, and more friends to play with.

RESPONSE-ABLE

Someone asks, "What do you really want?" and you panic. You've spent so much time and energy responding to imposed, external demands—from boss to family—that you're no longer *able to respond* to your real needs. In a tragic irony, your life may be completely in adult order—from low-rate mortgage to long-term insurance—but you're no longer *response-able.*

With amazing grace—amid the darkness our "adult agendas" have brought to this world—the Father has provided a saving beacon of light. Living right here among us, in fact, their faces shine forth with the saving truth of who we really are, where we come from, and where we're destined.

This is the ministry of the child, namely, to restore innocence to an awfully guilty world—and thereby, to make us once again *able to respond*, that is, *response-able,* even to God.

By no coincidence, this is precisely the ministry of Jesus: to restore innocence to a sin-infected world. That's why Jesus identifies with and enforces such a heart for children. It's why he speaks with such unprecedented fierceness against any attempt to assault their innocence. "If anyone should cause one of these little ones to lose his faith in me," he warned, "it would be better for that person to have a large millstone tied around his neck, and drowned in the sea" (Matt. 18:6).

Every dad knows that's a father's heart, to protect his kids. In fact, it's the heart of Father God for us, His children, which He gives to us dads in turn.

As adults, we work hard to draw closer to God so we can know His will. While helpful at times, this effort can allow the Tree of Knowledge to overshadow the Tree of Life.

Better than Obey and Work, God likes Show and Tell. In life's most important lessons, that is, He likes first to *show* us and only later *tell* us. He knows that at heart, we're children—even His own—and we learn best by example and experience.

That's what my stories here are about.

The ancient Greek culture of the New Testament esteemed the teaching of philosophers, who would mostly tell and not show. As a Jew, however, Jesus communicated truth more graphically. When questioned, like a good rabbi he often responded not with philosophical theories, bur rather, with engaging real-life stories, as parables with upending truth and unprecedented power.

In the child, that is, God has already shown us His desire for creation. Those with eyes to see this will welcome and celebrate the child among us, without having to be told to do so.

Meanwhile, in this fallen world, other forces blind us to God's design. The prince of Darkness doesn't want humanity to see the

Father's heart and the trail to His Kingdom on earth. He therefore hates children, who define that trail clearly and brightly—and are thereby the greatest living threat to the kingdom of darkness.

Today's media—from Saturday morning cartoon violence to prime time sex—reflect graphically this attack on children. **The devil's greatest triumph is to destroy a child's innocence, and thereby, the child's ministry among us.**

The enemy of God knows that sinful humanity in this fallen world labors under an overwhelming burden of shame. He wants us to remain stuck in that hopeless state. He knows the ministry of the child and thereby, that if we see children as God does, we'll remember the innocence we enjoyed with Him in the Garden. Hope will rise among us to be delivered from evil and thereby, determination to restore the Kingdom of God on earth as it is in heaven.

The child is no distraction amid adult tasks, no burden on adult freedom, no threat to adult agendas—that is, no more than Jesus. Indeed, as the bearer of innocence to a hopelessly sinful world, the child is the essential gateway to spiritual maturity and link to God's plan for humanity—the very avenue to His Kingdom rule in this world, the trailmarker pointing to the Tree of Life.

JESUS AND CHILDREN

Like Jesus, children are good news to a fallen world of bad news.

When we proud adults have dismissed and forgotten our hearts, however—when efforts to cover our shame have jealously mocked and crushed all innocence—we cut ourselves off from our true Father and become utterly lost in this world.

But He has not forsaken us. The clear and present evidence of His overwhelming grace is children, ever born again among us as a shining witness to our created purpose and destiny—their open, humble, and trusting hearts beckoning the gateway to God's rule on earth as it is in heaven.

Children whose natural—and indeed, sacred—humility and trust have not been assaulted, respond. They feel, and do something about it. They laugh, they cry. They experience life fully, and invite others into it. Like my son years ago, they leap into the icy surf, feel the great waves crashing against them, and shout to old hearts, "Come on in,

Daddy!"

What's more, kids respond truthfully.

In the old fable, con men trick a king into thinking they're tailors who have made him a majestic garment—when in fact they haven't made anything, and the king parades around naked in his "new clothing." While the adults pretend to approve in order not to disrespect the king and bring shame upon themselves, it's the child's voice which proclaims the simple truth, "The king has no clothes on!"—and thereby, restores the kingdom to sanity.

Such truth-tellers beckon the gateway to God's Kingdom. They're an unwelcome threat, however, to the kingdom of this world, where performance is the highest value and the shame of not measuring up is the primary motivator. In such a toxic environment, children "are to be seen and not heard"—as my grandmother often scolded me as a boy.

The child's innocence is thereby sacrificed to the adults' shame. The voice which beckons the Kingdom of Heaven—where God rules as King—is silenced.

Those who have forgotten the child, therefore, cannot be *response-able* adults, because they are not *able to respond* openly to their hearts—or thereby, to the Father.

In this world, being responsible means providing for your security. Its hallmark is industry, and its opposite, aimlessness. In the Kingdom of heaven, however, being responsible means literally being *able to respond* to God. Its hallmark is humility and its opposite, control. This means trusting that God has a plan for your life, and being *able to respond* as He reveals and moves in His Spirit to fulfill it.

PREPARE FOR GOD

John the Baptist, the voice of response-ability among Christians, therefore calls us not to increase our work for God, but rather, to "prepare the way" for God to work in and through us (Mt 3:1-3).

When we're not response-able to God, we can respond only to the world and its demand to measure up. Eventually, we grow tired of trying, even angry at failing. We either comply unto death and burn out, or rebel and drop out.

Today, at my age, I don't have the energy any more to feed this vicious cycle. I'm tired—literally—of responding to the world. I want to rest in my Father, to hear His call, trust His purposes, and be *able to respond* to Him with all the energy and focus He provides.

"Daddy, can you come out and play?"

Hold on. What's this?

Marvelously, while I'm holed up in my office behind the kitchen writing these very words about children, a small voice cries out from the other side of my door.

I hesitate; my article on fathering isn't finished yet. "What sort of… play...did you have in mind?" I call back tentatively through the closed door.

Engaged, the small voice brightens. "Do you wanna come to the zoo with me?"

I'm busted.

By the child—in fact, by Jesus—just as he chided the disciples of long ago, for not welcoming the child.

Chagrined, I sigh: *Welcome, Jesus! Would you please, please, open that door in my heart and welcome the boy—even the boy in me?*

Because children, you know, are a blessing.

"I'm ready!" I call back to the boy, smiling at last and shutting down my computer. "Let's go!"

At that, the door opens.

And together, we're off to see the lion.

Because a story about fathering—like life itself—isn't interrupted by the child.

It's fulfilled.

2

A Father Is Born

"You Lost Him to Me"

All at once, there was a shout from a man in the crowd. "Master, look at my son, I implore you, my only child!" (Luke 9:38 NEB)

THE FIRST AND ONLY CHILD for both of us in our forties, our son had been a surprisingly easy pregnancy, with no sickness for Mary and only minor discomfort. Our hopes for a similarly easy labor began to fade, however, when we discovered in the hospital delivery room that he was "posterior," or positioned backwards such that contractions pushed him against Mary's spinal cord with excruciating pain.

We had resolved to avoid a cesarean section. From the outset, however, the doctor feared serious stress to the baby through this ordeal of natural birth, and she declared that any consistently elevated heartbeat would dictate precisely such emergency measures. Reluctantly, we agreed. Yet, to the astonishment of doctor and nurses alike, the boy's heartbeat monitor showed no significant change throughout forty-two agonizing hours of labor.

The medical staff did not know, however, that we had established an elaborate prayer chain before going into the hospital. Like a frontline field commander to his supply corps, I was phoning out an update regularly between contractions. Furthermore, from the onset of labor-contraction after four-minute contraction, hour after hour—I had been laying hands on Mary's abdomen and praying very specifically.

I'M WITH YOU

First, I spoke directly to the boy in the womb. "Son," I said, "I know this is really hard, but many people are praying for you. If I could, I'd lift you out of it in a second, but I can't. I'll pray for you with all I've got. This is your battle, and you've got to stay strong and fight through it. **Whatever happens, I promise to stand here beside you and not go away. I'm your father.** I'm with you, and the Father of our forefathers has never left us."

And then, I would pray. "Mighty Jesus, victorious Lord Jesus, King of kings, Lord of lords, we give up to you. I have no power to win this battle, but all power is yours. In the name of Jesus, Father, pour out your Holy Spirit on this boy. Give him hope and determination and perseverance."

Finally, I would speak again to my son. "In the name of Jesus, I, your father, speak courage and strength to you!"

Throughout the ordeal, I was praying for Mary as well. Sometimes, I sobbed prayers through tears; at other times, I could only repeat words mechanically. Overall, however, I felt a distinct confidence.

After many hours of contractions, however, the doctor became concerned that Mary would have no strength left to push the baby out, and recommended vacuum suctioning. After a brief discussion, we agreed, and the doctor went ahead.

Standing by the hospital bed, my hands on its side railing, I looked up at the boy's heart monitor and watched in hypnotic rest the steadily flickering "135" base range that had reassured me for almost two days. Reaching to comfort Mary, I was jarred suddenly by an ugly, mucky *pop* sound.

"I can't hold the suction!" the doctor exclaimed nervously. My jaw dropped as I turned and saw the blood-streaked suction cup and handle in her hand. "It keeps breaking loose!"

I glimpsed a shock of dark hair emerging—and then disappearing back into the birth canal. For a second, the doctor hesitated, then spoke sharply to the attending nurse, who turned and left. Quickly, the doctor inserted the suction device again.

Startled by the sudden intensity of action, I glanced up and stared in disbelief. The boy's heartbeat had leapt to 215! Pale grey clothing swished ominously into the room and I turned to see several people in medical gowns closing in on us. Another, in surgical scrubs, rushed in, fastening a mask across his face.

What's happening? I cried out silently.

Beside me, the doctor worked feverishly with the suction handle. Another mucky *pop,* and the gowns closed the circle.

My stomach began to churn.

"He's not coming out!" a voice snapped. "The suction won't hold!"

COLD DARKNESS

A wave of cold darkness swept over me. *No! Jesus, no!* The words leapt into my mind and out of my mouth as the heaviness turned to dead weight. Suddenly, my knees began to buckle.

The gray mask stepped closer, and my head fell forward. Crumbling, I clutched desperately at the bed railing and fought to stay upright. "Jesus!" I whispered, wobbling as my knees hovered above the floor. "Jesus!"

"Wait . . . he's coming!" The words pierced the darkness over me like a laser beam. "He's coming! Here he comes . . ."

Determined to see, I grasped the railing and lurched upward.

Slowly, the shock of dark hair emerged. Then faster, the head, shoulders, and whole body slipped out. Quickly, the doctor handed the little body, limp and blue, to the nearest gown, and grasped the scissors.

"No wonder!" the doctor exclaimed. "The cord was wrapped around his legs, holding him back!"

Steadier now, I pulled myself up as the boy disappeared into the circle of gowns. Gathering myself, almost instinctively I lifted my arms and began circling the doctors, praising Jesus and praying aloud fiercely in my prayer language. After a moment, a bolt of courage struck me, and I stepped toward the grey huddle. Between busy cloth and prodding arms, I glimpsed a baby lying listlessly on a table in the center.

Disregarding hospital protocol, immediately I pressed closer, leaned over sideways, and slipped my right arm between two gowns. Feeling blindly for the boy's body, I prayed again.

"I'm your father and I'm with you," I began quickly.

Suddenly, a small swatch of wet hair touched my palm. "I'm . . . your father," I spoke again, choking as I held the tiny head in my hand, ". . . and the Father of our forefathers . . ."

But I could say no more. As the arms and gowns moved about me, I wept.

Minutes later, the boy emerged from the circle sleepy-eyed and wrapped securely in a small blanket. "Now at last, you get to hold him," the doctor announced to Mary, and set him in her arms.

With a deep, deep sigh, I leaned over the bed and put my arms around them both.

POWERLESS DAD, POWERFUL GOD

Even as we rejoiced at last over our son, Mary and I could not help asking God afterwards, "Why, with all our prayers, did we almost lose him?"

You did lose him, I sensed God's reply, about a week later:

> **You lost him to me.** *Your prayers as his father are more important than any other person's. But I wanted you to learn from the outset that it is I who saved the boy, not you. In order to experience this, you had to reach the point of seeing your son's life in the balance and not being able to pray at all.*
>
> *"This child is mine. I wanted you as soon as possible to recognize him as a son of the Father. He belongs to me. If he belonged to you, if words from your mouth were his saving power, he would have died trapped in the birth canal while you were passed out speechless on the hospital room floor.*
>
> *"You are his father, and I will honor your prayers*

for him. But you are both my sons. My purposes for
him are greater than you can know, and with your
cooperation I will see to it that he fulfills my calling.

With these words, "the Father from whom all fatherhood in heaven
and on earth receives its true name" called me forth into the adventure
(Ephes. 3:14NIV footnote).

3

The Cry for Daddy[3]
Awakening the Father

*For the Spirit that God has given you does not
make you slaves and cause you to be afraid; instead,
the Spirit makes you God's children, and by the Spirit's power we cry out to God, "Father! My Father!"*
(Romans 8:15,16)

AFTER A YEAR, THE LATE-NIGHT NURSINGS were beginning
to exhaust Mary. Compassionately, I determined to find someone to
help her. This helper, I knew, would need a special heart for children,
even for our son—and of course, would have to live nearby, if not
right here in....

At that, a brilliant but unsettling insight struck me:

It's time for Dad to get in on the action.

I'll cut to the chase. I didn't look forward to being awakened
randomly at night. I admired Mary's perseverance, but I'm a heavy
sleeper. "I don't know how you do it," I'd said often.

Now it was time to find out.

I confess I balked at nighttime feedings partly because my son
always awoke crying out, "Mommy!" I felt like a second-fiddle
mom—and not a very good one at that. Nevertheless, I girded my

loins for the challenge, and decided to surprise Mary by telling her the good news at bedtime.

SURPRISE FOR MOM

Earlier that night, I had prepared a bottle and set it on my night stand. As we got into bed and she dropped exhausted onto her pillow, I knew I'd have to act quickly.

"Honey, I have a surprise for you!" I announced brightly.

"Huh?" she murmured, eyes closed and voice trailing off. "Whass...that?"

"I'm going to do the nighttime feedings."

At that—with a bolt of energy known best to mama bears—Mary burst awake and leapt up, eyes flaming. "You're *what*?"

"I said, 'I'm going to take care of the nighttime feedings'. Now, don't worry. I made up a bottle and it's right here beside me. When he wakes up, I'll just....well, just put it in his mouth. You need some rest."

That last sentence got her attention. Sighing as the bolt fizzled, she yielded—unable to muster the energy to protest. "Well, alright," she allowed, falling back and turning over. "Just be sure you do it right."

"Right"? **I wondered, suddenly uneasy.** *How can you do it wrong? All you do is wait til his mouth is open and stick it in!*

Graciously attributing her lack of confidence to sleep deprivation, I nodded. "Sure, honey, I'll do it right. You just get a good rest— you've earned it!"

Suddenly, one detail leapt into my mind. "Oh, wait," I interjected quickly, before she could fall asleep, "I may need your help. You know I'm a heavy sleeper, so if I don't wake up when he cries, just give me a little nudge."

"Mmm-hm," Mary allowed, and drifted off.

Pleased with my plan, I congratulated myself and settled under the covers at last for a good night's sleep.

It was not to be.

In a flash—or so it seemed—a sharp elbow jabbed my side and

jolted me awake.

"He's awake and crying!" Mary announced, with an urgency that pre-empted any little nudge. With a start, she turned to get out of bed—then paused. "You said you have a bottle?"

Blinking and gathering myself, I yawned. "Uh-huh," I murmured, pulling the covers higher. As I did, the all-too-familiar cry rang out from across the hall:

"MOMMMYYY!!!"

She was right. The boy was indeed awake and crying.

SURPRISE FOR DAD

Half asleep yet, I turned courteously to inform Mary that she was being summoned—only to find her turned over and, by all appearances, fast asleep. Dismayed, I remembered my "surprise" for her—which now seemed more surprising to me.

I confess I was not greatly motivated by this cry for "Mommy." After all, I did have something to do with all this—even if it *was* the easy part. Sighing nevertheless, I pulled myself out of bed and gripped the bottle determinedly.

Maybe it won't be so bad after all, I told myself, and stumbled into the darkness.

With a deep breath, I shuffled across the hall, hesitated, then drew myself up and stepped pro-actively into the boy's bedroom. "Daddy's here!" I announced sharply. "It's OK!"

To my pleasant surprise, the room fell silent.

Well, that wasn't so hard! I thought, and walked confidently toward the crib. As I bent over the railing, however, the boy looked up. Scrutinizing my face in the faint moonlight for a long moment, he turned toward the outreached bottle—and realized that this was not at all what he had ordered.

"MOMMMYYYY!!!" Shattering my eardrums along with my ego, the cry blasted forth with renewed vigor.

Startled, I paused, looked back wistfully over my shoulder toward the object of this cry—then at last, turned back to my son and inhaled again with resolve. Gingerly, I reached down, lifted him up—and when he opened his mouth to shout again, stuck the bottle in.

BACK TO BED...NOT

A few slushy, squeaky sucks later, the boy fell asleep once again astride my shoulder. Gratefully, I returned him to his crib, and tiptoed quickly back to bed. With a sigh, I lay back. *That was harder than I thought—but at least it's over.* Gratefully, I closed my eyes and....

And again, out of nowhere, The Elbow struck. Just seconds later—or so it once again seemed. By daybreak, I had forgotten how many times I struggled through that same taxing routine. My best guess would be, Too many.

Sure, I wanted to get close to my son. But I'm a heavy sleeper, and in the nights to follow, The Elbow and relentless cries for "Mommy!" were not helpful invitations to bond.

Soon, I began bargaining with the Lord. I prayed. I begged. I was ready to deal. *Please, Lord, make him sleep! It's better for the baby, after all. I'll pray an extra hour a day. I'll increase my tithe!*

But still the cry for "Mommy!" went on. And on.

Night after night, bottle after bottle, I pushed on through the cries for "Mommy"—dutifully, if not lovingly.

Eventually, however, I began to enjoy just holding my little son. Before long, I was praying for him, even singing my prayers quietly at times. On a few especially tough nights, when the bottle and Daddy's singing didn't do the job, we walked out on the patio under the stars and talked about moons and raisin bread and raccoons and space ships.

And then late one night after going to bed, it happened.

Lost thankfully in heavy sleep, I stirred as a strange sound tapped lightly on my ear.

"Daa-dee..."

My eyes flickered open, closed again. Shifting, I reached to pull the covers higher.

"DA-DEE! DAA-DEEEEE!"

Bold and full-throated, like a mighty bugle the small voice pierced the dark morning stillness.

MY MAN

My eyes exploded open. Springing from the bed, I raced across the hall into my son's room, bent over his crib, and scooped him up in my arms. "That's my man!" I cried out, laughing and lifting him high above my head. "Haleluia! That's my man!"

"What's…going on in there?" Mary called out anxiously from back in our bedroom. "I didn't even wake you up, and you're already over there making all that noise! Is the baby OK?"

Sheepishly, I lowered a confused and bleary-eyed boy to my chest. "Yes, yes, the baby's fine," I called back. "I'm not sure…exactly what's going on. But…it's OK. I mean, it's good."

I held my son against me at last and smiled. "It's good," I whispered, bouncing now and shaking my head, amazed. "Real good."

That night, everything changed. Before then, as soon as he fell asleep, I would put him in the crib and dash gratefully back to bed.

Now, I took my time. Long after the steady tump-tump of his heart on my shoulder told me he was asleep, we walked together in the quiet of the night. Not just around his room, but down the hallway, around kitchen, dining room, and office, out onto the patio and back again.

When finally I returned him to the crib asleep, it struck me: What, indeed, stirred and even leapt within me when I first heard my son cry out "Daa-dee!"?

Certainly, my joy came partly from waiting so long for him to acknowledge the bond between us. And yet, when I had rejoiced fully and Mary was asleep again, I lay in bed staring at the ceiling in awe, gripped by something deeper.

Clearly, what happened was no sequence of logical decisions, as, "I hear a shout. That is my son's voice. He is calling for his daddy. I am his daddy. Therefore, I will get out of bed and go to him."

Not at all. My son cried out for me by name, and immediately some inner launching switch flipped to rocket me toward him.

What in the world's going on here, Father?

And then I knew: **I was identifying with the cry of my son. In his baby's voice, I heard something I recognized in myself.**

I now believe we all harbor that cry deep within our hearts, awaiting the night. It's the primal human cry for security and saving power in a dark and broken world: "Save me, Daddy!"

TOWERING STRENGTH

As another father puts it,

> Kids respect a father's towering strength just as they respect all other big things: giants, dragons, dinosaurs, and whales. But with a difference. Dad is so close that they needn't be intimidated by his strength; they can use it as a refuge; they can use him for protection.

> A child enlists superheroes as allies against the monsters and bad guys in his world. But probably even more useful to a four-year-old than Batman and Super Woman is a father who is right there when he's needed to punch out a whale or banish brontosaurs from the hall closet.[4]

In fact, the cry for "Daddy!" within us all is the fountainhead of our faith, as it stirs the heart of Father God like no other—even as my son's cry catapulted me toward him. As Paul told the Romans in the opening Scripture above, it's the ministry of Holy Spirit in this present age to enable that cry—so the greatest Super Hero of all, Father God Himself, can demonstrate His saving power to His children.

Before Mary and I were married, my best friend—a father of two—told me, "Nothing will help you understand the love of God like having a child of your own."

He was right.

May we men dare to listen to the cry for "Daddy!" within our own hearts, so we can hear it in our children.

4

"Why Do You Love Your Son?"
The Heart Connection

And a voice came from heaven: "You are my Son, whom I love; with you I am well pleased."

At once the Spirit sent him out into the desert and he was in the desert forty days, being tempted by Satan. (Mark 1:9-12NIV)

SOON AFTER THE TENSION OF FIRST-TIME FATHERING began to wear off—the nightly is-he-still-breathing? visits to the crib, the fears of dropping the squiggly baby—I found myself praising God for this new life He had placed in our care. One morning, in fact, an overwhelming love surged into my heart, and I could only fall on my knees in thanksgiving.

In that moment, as I knelt on the carpet in my study, I knew that no matter what the powers of the world might throw at my son, I would defend him with my life. A strange mixture of joy, strength, and then fear swept over me. "Father!" I cried out, overwhelmed. "I love this boy more than I've ever loved anyone or anything in this world!"

At that, a question popped into my mind: *Why do you love him?*

Startled—and frankly unsure—I paused and wondered. Is it because he performs so well and does so much work for me? Does he do anything that makes me look good in the eyes of other men? Make straight A's so I feel proud at the PTA meeting? Hit a home run to win the game?

"No," I laughed out loud; "all he 'does for me' is fill up his diapers and cry all night!"

I hesitated. Then why *do* I love him?

Knitting my brow, I sat quietly. After a moment, it hit me. "I guess," I offered, shrugging my shoulders in surrender, "...because he's my son."

That's all? I sensed immediately.

BECAUSE HE'S MY SON

Again I hesitated, then sighed with a smile, nodding. "Yes, Father—that's all. I love him so much it scares me. Just...because he's my son."

It was not the right answer. It was the only answer.

Waiting, I "heard" nothing else, as if the Father were letting that truth sink into my heart. As I sat there smiling, it did.

And then, like a bolt, the words leapt into my mind: *And why do I love you, Gordon?*

Patently obvious, the answer nevertheless terrified me. In my emotional "background," the entire superstructure of my accomplished adult life shuddered and creaked ominously.

Kneeling frozen in fear, I realized how much I had invested my life in trying to please God with my 'performance' offerings. Suddenly, my good grades in school, my great insights and well-crafted sermons, my books, all my "sacrifices" to prove my worth to God, were but a monument to my distrusting His love—which now wavered on a fragile ledge of crumbling rock.

As from an earthquake in my heart, I trembled.

I guess...you love me... because I'm your son.

At that, the foundation burst at last, and crumbled. Both startling and reassuring, the truth seized me.

For some time, I knelt quietly.

Eventually, I wondered: **Could I really trust God to love me—**

indeed, would I remain His son?—if I stopped doing all these things to earn His favor?

Praying, I realized Jesus was urging me, even as the Pharisees: "Go, and learn what this means: 'I desire mercy, and not sacrifice.' For I came not to call the righteous, but sinners" (Matt. 9:13RSV).

In that moment He was calling me:

> *My son, my son, rest in me! I love you just be-cause you're mine, created in my image. I love you so much it scares me—because you might trash my love by setting me up as a tightwad tyrant and trying religiously to earn it—when in fact, it's yours, simply to receive! Please, son, receive my love. Without it, you'll be easily misled to counterfeits.*

God, I realized, had never demanded I do as He says in order to gain His love. Rather, He had given me His love so I *can* do as He says.

"Love comes from God," as John declared (1 John 4:7). Now, He was asking me to believe that and receive it. For my own welfare, certainly—but more. If a father doesn't receive Father God's love for himself, he has none to give his child.

When Father God parted heaven to baptize and proclaim "This is my son, in whom I am well pleased," how much ministry had Jesus performed?

None.

Was the Father saying to His son Jesus, "Now that you've cast out demons, healed the sick, raised the dead, out-preached the Pharisees, raised up disciples, and performed so successfully—at last I love you and am pleased with you!"?

No.

DAD'S LOVE PREPARES

Rather, the Father was providing for His Son's ministry. Immediately after proclaiming His joy in Jesus, in fact, the Father sends Him out into the desert to battle Satan. That gift of His Father's love provided Jesus the basic foundation for any later accomplishment in behalf of the Father's Kingdom—and upon which to battle successfully any resistance from the enemy.

He was saying,

> *I'm calling you to engage and defeat the very powers of Hell, and you need to be equipped for my victory.*

> *These powers of darkness and death want to sabotage your destiny, primarily by separating you from me. When times get tough, they'll try to make you think I don't love you, that in fact I've abandoned you.*

> *First and foremost, therefore, you must know that I love you, that I delight in you as my Son. If you don't know this, the enemy can seduce your heart away from me. But as you walk securely in relationship with me as your Father, we're as one, and my victory is assured both in and through you.*

Father God's announcing He's "pleased" with His Son prepared Jesus to resist Satan's temptations. Similarly, a dad's blessing prepares his child for the battles of life—and the true Father's victory.

Your blessing gives your child confidence and motivation to do what you say.

"Many approach the teachings of Jesus as just *another form of the Law*," as Pastor Bill Johnson of Bethel Church in Redding, CA, notes. "To most He just brought a new set of rules. (But) grace is different from the Law in that the favor comes before the obedience. Under grace the commandments of the Lord come fully equipped with the ability to perform them…to those who hear from the heart. *Grace enables what it commands*" (sic).[5]

After the revelation in that prayer for my son, I wanted him to presume upon my love, to take it for granted. I don't want his striving anxiously to please me in hopes of earning my love. Otherwise, when sooner or later he realizes that I don't have all that he needs, he'll hate me as if I were withholding it—then act out in ways that ultimately sabotage his manhood.

This, then, is my prayer: *Father, give me the love my son needs from me.*

It's harmful not to give a son what he needs to fulfill his calling. But it's demonic to criticize him for not "living up to his potential" while withholding from him the love that would enable him to do it. As Jesus charged the Pharisees, that's laying an unbearable burden on him "without lifting a finger" to help (Matt. 23:4).

Do you know your Father loves you—no matter how badly you mess up? If you don't, it's hard for you to love your child, especially when he or she messes up.

Kids do mess up, you know.

Or have you forgotten?

If so, I remind you: When a boy makes a mistake, he fears that others will shame him. He needs his dad to speak to him not just the truth of his mistake, but the grace of knowing he's still loved by his daddy. That's what allows his heart to stay engaged, face his mistakes honestly, and do better next time.

A good way to stand with the boy in his mistake, so he doesn't shut down from its shame, is simply to tell him about your own mistakes. "You didn't get it right this time, son," you can say, "but you know what? Neither did I when I was your age. I fact, even now there are things I try hard to get right, but don't. So let's see if we can figure out how to try this again and do it better."

Sure, for Dad this means being real and risking shame. But that's exactly what you want the boy to learn. In fact, that's how God showed love to us, sending Jesus to die so shamefully on the Cross. In fact, Jesus' Father met Him there, and turned what the world tried to hide into the cornerstone of saving grace.

Once, a man came to me angry that his son took the family car and put a lot more miles on it than he allowed. "Can you believe it?" the father fumed, "when I confronted him with the evidence on the odometer, he never even said he was sorry or asked me to forgive him for doing what I told him not to!"

"That's really frustrating," I allowed. "I can understand why you're angry."

I paused to affirm this man. In that moment, though, I sensed something amiss in his fury. Praying quickly—*Father, this is a little dicey, so lead me on here*—I asked him a simple question: "If you're a normal man, you've disappointed and hurt your son at times. When was the last time you told your son you were sorry for that and asked him to forgive you?"

TAUGHT BY EXAMPLE

The man drew back, offended. "What do you mean, 'ask my son to forgive me'?" he snapped. "I'm the father here!"

OK Father, I prayed under my breath, *stand with me in this!*

"That's exactly what I mean," I explained. "You're the father. You're the one who shows your son by example what a man is like. **If you've never asked your son's forgiveness for something you've done, you've taught him by example that men don't own up to their faults.** When he doesn't own up to over-using your car, he's just being like you. Don't expect him to say something you want to hear when you haven't shown him how."

The fact that I'm still alive to write this story tells you that this brother was man enough to let the sword of truth cut to his own wound unto healing. "Yeah," he confessed, dropping his eyes. "That's true. My dad could never say he was sorry to me for anything. I don't want to keep this thing going another generation."

A dad doesn't lose authority by humbling himself before the son in order to teach grace.

He demonstrates it.

That's because, like Father God, your authority with your child lies not in your mind to punish, but in your heart to bless.

5

Stung by an Angel
Healing Father-Blindness

In those days, people will no longer say, "The fathers ate the sour grapes, and the children's teeth are set on edge." (Jeremiah 31:29 NIV)

IT HAD BEEN A LONG, BUSY DAY, and I decided to combine fathering with work by editing my teaching tapes as my three-year-old son played beside me on the carpet with his trucks. Eventually, I decided to take a break, and turned to the boy.

"Daddy needs to rest a bit and read the newspaper," I declared, disappearing into my easy chair behind the Sports page. "So don't touch those tapes."

I was well into a cliff-hanger story about a last-minute Lakers' basket, when to my surprise I heard a strange rustling sound below and in front of me—definitely not like a truck. Puzzled, I glanced over my paper.

To my shock, there was my carefully positioned-for-edit tape pulled out of the cassette like scrambled brown spaghetti. My hours of work now lay strung around the floor, lost.

"What are you *doing?*" I exclaimed angrily, tossing aside the paper and leaping to my feet. "I thought I told you not to touch those tapes!"

Startled and afraid, the boy jumped up and froze solid.

Look at all my teachings! I sighed in disgust. *He's disobeyed me and now he's going to pay for it!*

Grimacing at the dark mish-mash of tape, I shook my head. With a mixture of dismay and determination, I then turned sternly to the boy.

BOY AND GIANT

At this point, I need to push the PAUSE button and set the scene.

Here was a three-foot-tall boy standing before an almost-six-foot-tall man. The man is angry at the boy, who has no exit or advocate. To grasp the impact, imagine yourself a six-foot-tall man looking up at another man towering over you at twice your height—fully twelve feet tall. That's two feet taller than a basketball net. Proportionately, he's got you by several hundred pounds and he's angry.

At you.

OK. Now we push the button and continue.

* PLAY *

Eyes wide, the little boy stood shaking before me. As I glared at him, suddenly, strangely, a tiny but sharp sensation nicked the side of my chin, like a mild bee sting, diverting my attention. "Stung by an angel" is the only way I could think later to describe it.

In that brief but eternal moment, a seeming conversation was taking place in my heart.

What do you see? Matter-of-fact but deliberate, the question entered my mind.

That's easy. I see my teaching tapes strewn all over the carpet!

Again, quickly, the sting on my chin. And again, the question, more deliberately this time: *What do you see?*

I see my teaching tape all over the floor! I huffed—more deliberately this time.

Yet again, the sting. This time strong enough to push my head away from the tape to see....

What do you see?

Sharply now, the question drew me up.

I swallowed deeply as the tape faded and I saw....*a little boy.*

What do you see in his body? the response shot back.

He's...he's kind of stiff and...well, I see... fear... in his eyes... and in his body.

What's he afraid of? The options came rapid-fire: *A thief climbing in the window? A lion breaking through the door? An earthquake shaking the house?* Sternly, the sense paused, as if hovering.

TREMBLING BOY

An uneasiness seized my stomach and I sucked in deeply. *Well... no,* I managed, as a hot fear began seeping into me. *I mean,....he's afraid of... well,...of me.*

Exhaling gingerly, I looked again **at a small boy trembling in fear beneath the giant man above him.**

In that moment at last, I knew him.

Years, even generations of pain burst as through a dam and flooded my heart. At once, I fell on my knees. With arms outstretched, I reached for my son. "I...I'm so sor-"

"MOMMMYYY!!!" he shouted out, jumping back. "MOMMMYYY!!!"

That wasn't what I wanted to hear.

* PAUSE *

You thought maybe if Dad just got humble, the boy would open his heart? Hold on. This story is about fathering. It's no fairy tale. It's an adventure.

Four years earlier, when he was born, I had talked to Mary about boys. "We're both male," I said. "We're going to get into it sometimes—disagreements, arguments, and all. I know you love him, but **I need to ask you not to rescue the boy from the man. Don't save the son from his father.**

"I suppose it's easy for women to think men can't settle their differences without guns and fights and all, but I need you to trust me on this. I want to be real with him and work things out together, just the two of us."

Eyes narrowed and brow furrowed, Mary sat thinking. "OK," she allowed finally. And that was that.

At least, I hoped so.

In any case, now it was time to find out.

MOMMY EAGLE

Note: When her child cries out for her, a good mommy comes, even as on wings of an eagle.

* PLAY *

When Mary heard the walls reverberate with her son's distress call, she flew into the living room—and drew up as she saw me on my knees, hands outstretched to our son, who was still shaking with fear.

Turning to her, I forced a smile. "Thank...you...for...coming," I spoke very, very deliberately—then glanced at the boy and lifted my eyes back toward where she'd been.

Catching my drift, the momma eagle paused, uncertain. Then, with a quick but firm "you'd-better-be-right" scowl in my direction, she walked to the boy, bent down, and gave him a hug. By the grace of God, with a faithful and patently super-natural effort to overcome her mother-instinct, she then pulled herself away, turned and left.

The boy's gaze followed her. I confess, so did mine—and it occurred to me to ask her to stay.

In that moment's opportunity, however, I shuffled my knees awkwardly, seized my son and threw my arms around him. He struggled to get away, but I held him tightly, refusing to let go. "I'm... so, so...sorry," I stumbled. "When I was a boy, I...."*Father, help!* "I don't want you to have to... I mean, ...I'm...I'm so sorry I was angry at you like that. I love you so much. I don't ever want to scare you like that again. Please forgive me!"

At that, I gave him a strong hug and eased my grip—and at last, the boy burst into tears. "Standing" on my knees, I held him as he sobbed, shaking in my arms.

How long we "stood" there together, I can't say. I can only say that when we finally parted, I was overcome with a churning fear and shame that led me directly to my prayer closet for a long time.

There, I saw the disarming truth. From the boy's perspective, Daddy was playing with the tape. A boy wants most to do what Daddy does—and my son was simply wanting to do what I was doing.

He just wanted to be like me, and I was punishing him for it. If I didn't want him to play with the tape, I should never have "played" with it myself in front of him without giving him a chance to join me.

Overcome with shame and remorse, I led him later to my trashcan and told him he could dig out any old tapes from it. "Go ahead and tear them apart or whatever," I told him. "It's OK. Just put it all back in the can when you're finished."

THERAPY FUND

No matter how hard I prayed, however, I just couldn't shake the guilt. Forget the boy's college fund; it was time to start a therapy fund. By the time I came out of my office, I didn't care what happened, as long as I didn't have to look my wife in the eye ever again.

I did, however, want to sleep that night. Before daring to enter our bedroom, I waited until the boy was asleep in his room and Mary had gone to bed and turned out the lights.

Carefully, I sidestepped into our room, slipped quickly under the covers, and lay back on my pillow with a measured sigh of relief.

"So how did it go?"

"Wh-what?" I burst out, my eyes leaping open. *Father, help! How am I going to deal with this?* "I mean, uh, how did what go?"

"How did it go with the boy?"

"'The boy'?" I echoed matter-of-factly, my gaze fixed on the ceiling.

"Yes," Mary said, now with more than a hint of concern at my waffling. "What happened after I left you two together?"

"Well, sure—after you left us together," I stalled. "Thank you,... for leaving us together."

But it was too late.

HE CRIED

"OK, I'll tell you," I blurted out finally. Sitting up, I turned on the nightstand light. Determined to take it like a man, I looked Mary in the eye. "It was awful. I destroyed him. I crushed his heart and he cried so bad I could hardly hold him."

Confused, Mary did a double-take, and sat up immediately. "He cried?"

"Yes, he cried. He cried awful. I mean, it was terrible. What I did just crushed him. I said I was sorry and asked him to forgive me, but he cried like I've never seen him cry before, just sobbing and shaking all over and...."

"Haleluia!" Mary shouted out, bounding from the bed and dancing around the bedroom. Beaming, she raised her hands in praise. "Thank you, Lord Jesus, thank you!"

Startled, I drew back. "What do you...I mean, what are you doing?" I asked.

"He cried!" she exclaimed. "He got it out! That means he's OK!"

"I don't get it," I offered, baffled. "How can...."

"Listen," Mary said, taking my hand and shaking her head in dismay. And then with a playful smile, "He's not like you. He doesn't stuff his feelings and stew over things. **He felt afraid and hurt, and he cried. It's as simple as that. Trust me, if he sobbed like you said, it's gone, done, forgotten.**"

Sighing happily, Mary squeezed my hand. "Now turn out the light and let's get some sleep."

Uneasily, I squeezed back. Shaking my head in disbelief, I reached uncertain for the light switch.

* PAUSE *

Awhile after this event, I had finished teaching at a men's conference and asked for responses.

"May I speak, please?" From the congregation, a hand went up slowly but deliberately—and a white-haired man leaned into his cane to stand.

Delighted to welcome an elder brother, I stepped back graciously and gestured the man to go ahead. "Yes, please do speak to us," I urged.

Turning on his cane with a shuffle, he stood for a long moment looking over the audience of men. "You don't need to know how old I am," he declared, "but I'm in my 80's. I just want to say this: Whatever you don't forgive your father for, you'll do to your son."

Pausing, sweeping his gaze once more around the room, he turned back to me, nodded with a "Thank you," and sat down.

Utter silence fell upon us all.

* PLAY *

The next morning, I eased into the kitchen where my son sat looking at the Sunday comics over his cereal while Mary was putting some dishes away.

AMAZING GRACE

"Want some more honey on your corn flakes?" I offered the boy. "Maybe some cookies? How about a slice of that leftover pizza?"

"Mm-mm," the boy nodded absently, turning a page. "Hey Daddy," he called suddenly, bursting out laughing and pointing to the paper. "Look what the dinosaur does to the cave man!"

Unsure, I ventured ahead. "What...does the dinosaur do, son?"

"Come over here with me and look, Daddy! This is so funny!"

I went over there with him, and when I looked, it really was funny. In fact, we both laughed together. As we did, I saw Mary smiling.

"Amazing grace," the old song goes—freely translated—

...how sweet the sound

That saved a dad like me.

I once was lost, but now I'm found,

Was blind, but now I see.

6

Captain Donald Duck
Toward New Covenant Fathering

Fathers, don't exasperate your children by coming down hard on them. Take them by the hand and lead them in the way of the Master. (Ephes. 6:4TMB)

FIVE THIRTY IN THE AFTERNOON is not a good time to enter a supermarket. But Mommy needed a few last ingredients for supper, so Daddy and kindergartner son were drafted for the task.

At the moment of call, the two of us were enjoying a Donald Duck cartoon. There, the dubious "hero" had declared himself captain of an old rowboat and commissioned nephews Huey, Dewey, and Louie as Lieutenants. Amid misguided orders from Uncle Donald and much saluting and regrouping among the boys, the hapless vessel had struck a rock and was spouting water.

But larger orders prevailed. Leaving Captain Donald to sputter in his demise, we left home port and set sail for the supermarket together.

Sure enough, as we passed through the swooshing glass doors, a rush of voices engulfed us amid busy, anxious, end-of-the-workday crowds. To save time and to engage the boy in the mission, I decided to ask him to get one of the list items himself.

A large yellow heap of bananas caught my eye as we entered the store, and I pointed him toward the fruit and vegetable section. As loudly as possible amid the din without drawing undue attention to myself, I spoke out, "Go right over there and get a bunch of about 4 or 5 bananas!"

Turning to fulfill my own orders in the milk section, I was startled to hear the boy shout back loud and clear, "YES, SIR!"

CRISP SALUTE

Looking back, I saw him draw up to attention, click his heels, and offer a crisp salute.

At once all chatter within hearing distance of the artichoke display stopped, and a hush fell immediately over the entire fruit and vegetable community. Fathers, mothers, authoritative adults of all sorts froze in amazement. All eyes turned in astonishment to the boy standing stiffly at attention salute, and then to me.

"H-How do you get him to do *that*?" one woman exclaimed at last, her red-circled eyes testifying to her own failure as she restrained a small boy in her hand.

"Well, actually," I managed, "I… didn't…I mean, I really don't make him do things like that."

Startled myself, and puzzled, I drew up—and suddenly remembered Captain Donald!

"Ah!" I exclaimed at last to my now-captive audience, "We were just watching a Donald Duck cartoon at home where the kids were saluting him." Shrugging, I lifted my hands in surrender. "The boy's just play acting what he saw in the movie."

Forcing an apologetic smile, I turned to my son. "At ease," I called out sheepishly. "Thanks. Just…go get the bananas."

Their cherished hopes for Instant Child Control dashed, like a punctured inner tube the crowd sighed collectively, and turned back in frustration to the spinach and apples.

TRUCKS AND TESTOSTERONE

Anyone who's ever experienced a kindergartener knows **that desire for a magic wand to make the child cooperate.** That same population, however, knows how elusive such order and peace can be.

This issue became graphically real to me just after my son's first birthday, when we began taking walks together around the block.

Months earlier—with absolutely no coaching from me—one of his first words had been "truck."

"Is it in the testosterone?" Mary asked, amazed.

I don't know. I only know that, as a normal tactile, concrete-thinking toddler, he wanted to go out in the street and touch every truck that passed. As I held one hand, he would lean and reach out his other hand, straining toward the street, and cry, "Truck! Truck!"

Eventually, the tugging increased until I had to kneel beside him on the sidewalk and put restraining arms around him. Immediately, an urge arose within me—was it testosterone?—to spank him and shout "No!"

And yet, as the truck whooshed by us, my fear was lost in confusion. I found myself not only holding my son protectively from the street, but drawing him affectionately to myself.

Restraint merged with love—and I balked.

ARROWS OF SHAME

Immediately, arrows of shame struck: *Don't wimp out! Take control and show your strength! You're the father. If you love him, hit him and say No! Be a man and do your job! You're supposed to force him to obey—it's clearly for his own good. Do you want him to get killed by a car? It'll be your fault if he does.*

Still, I hesitated. His impulses were not malicious or even mischievous. Indeed, how could I punish a boy for wanting to touch a truck? As Mary suggested, it's in his makeup as a boy. **The issue, rather, was somehow to separate the good desire to touch a truck from the bad practice of running out into the street.**

His tender year-old sensibility couldn't see any larger danger, nor appreciate any larger agenda behind Daddy's hitting him. His little mind could only reason, "Daddy and I are having fun walking together. Why is he hitting me for wanting to do something fun?" I didn't want him to be afraid of being punished for having fun.

More important, I didn't want shame to overshadow our relationship. "If I'm not doing anything wrong," he might reason, "why is Daddy so angry at me? Doesn't he like me anymore?"

Certainly, I don't want my son to get hit by a truck. But the bargain was absurd: Should a boy have to give up Daddy's love in order to be safe? Indeed, for a child, safety itself is defined by Daddy's love.

The man who hasn't looked honestly at his own boyhood longing for Daddy's love can't recognize himself in such thoughts and may discount them as sentimental and unmanly. In shutting down his father-longing, he trades Father God's love for the more apparent security of doing it the way his dad and other men do it.

Because Dad models masculinity to every boy, often when a man becomes a father himself, he fears being unmanly for not punishing his children like Dad did. He thereby abdicates his destiny as Father God's son for his earthly father's approval.

On the sidewalk, meanwhile, I could only pray, *Father God, help! You know I want to be a good father. I want to make my son feel safe and loved. **I want him to fear the moving truck, not me.** Show me how to do it!*

As the little boy protested, wriggling in my arms, I heard no answer but an aching love in my heart.

BIG OWWY!

Uncertain but deliberate, I hugged him firmly and looked him in the eye. "Daddy loves his boy," I said. "Truck big! BOOM in street!" I grimaced dramatically. "Hurt boy! Big OWWY! Stay on sidewalk with Daddy. Daddy loves his boy. Daddy carry boy on street. No owwy. Boy happy. Daddy happy." At that, the wiggling stopped—*was it just because there were no trucks at that moment?*—and we walked on.

Soon afterwards, I spotted a parked truck, and pointed to it.

"Truck! Truck!" he shouted excitedly, stretching for it as always. Immediately, I picked him up and carried him over to stand by the curb next to the truck.

"Daddy loves his boy." I said, squeezing him gently. "Daddy carry boy to truck. Truck stopped. Truck OK, no street. Boy touch truck." I shifted him into one arm and extended the other toward the truck to encourage him.

Hesitantly, reverently, my son reached out and caressed the truck's red tail-light as I held him in my arms.

Thereafter on our walks, whenever I picked him up and stepped out into the crosswalk, I held him especially close to me to communicate both love and protection. "Daddy loves his boy," I would say. "Daddy carry boy on street. No owwy. Daddy happy. Boy happy."

After a few times, he got the idea. When a truck or car approached, without my saying a word he stopped walking ahead and drew close to me. As he held onto my leg, I knelt down and hugged him, and together we enjoyed watching the car whoosh by and even making our very own "VRRROOOMM!" engine noises.

I continued to lift him up at corners and tell him, "Daddy loves his boy, Daddy carry boy street," as I lifted him to cross the intersections. Eventually, we came to one corner, and to my pleasant surprise— without my saying a word and before I could bend over—he turned to me and lifted his hands: "Daddy carry!" he exclaimed

Hallelujah! Yes! I cried out in my spirit. *That's what we're looking for. Trust in the father, protection from the moving vehicle, joy in anticipating another parked truck.*

Yet the true test was yet to come.

Several days later, we were playing with his tricycle in the front yard, and the phone rang. Intending to jump inside and take the call only for a second, I said, "Daddy go phone. Boy stay on grass." The call turned out to be engaging, and after a minute I caught myself in fear and raced back out front.

Thankfully, the boy was simply standing on the sidewalk, looking out at the street. A few cars were passing by and I was about to shout at him—but a compelling sense of restraint came over me. Instead, I ran out on tiptoes close enough to where I could grab him if necessary, prayed, and waited to see what he would do.

He hesitated—I could almost see his mind turning over the options—and then finally turned back toward the house. As he climbed onto his tricycle, he saw me. Straining to seem casual, I walked over, and with a measured sigh knelt down and hugged him.

"Daddy loves his boy," I said. "Boy stay on grass and sidewalk. No owwy street!"

Matter-of-factly, he nodded. "Daddy carry boy street."

"Yes, that's right," I said, smiling and holding him closely. "Daddy carry boy street."

LESSON LEARNED AND TAUGHT

But hold on. There's more.

A year and a half later, my son would still stop at street corners for me to pick him up. In fact, far from running amok for lack of "godly discipline," he internalized the lesson deeply enough to see the larger picture beyond his own safety.

In that season, one day Mary came home with him from play group at a small meeting house set back from the street maybe 25 feet and up a small incline. When the program had finished, she reported, our son and many of the other children ran out of the classroom. The mothers raced out fearfully after them, but Mary did not.

As she casually gathered her purse and materials, one frantic mother passing by spoke sharply to her. "Aren't you afraid your boy will run out in the street?"

Mary was not—at least, not until this frightened mother stirred her sense of guilt. Hurrying outside with the others, she was surprised to see our son standing on the sidewalk calling anxiously to several children who were already at the edge and moving toward the curb. "NO!" he was shouting. "Stay on the sidewalk! Come back! Stop! Don't go in the street!"

What can you do but worship?

I believe this process shows how Father God deals with our often thoughtless but dangerous behavior.

I wanted to change my son's behavior. **When I surrendered my goal to Jesus and invested instead in our relationship, the boy changed his behavior—seeking the best for himself, and even for others.**

True father-love—that is, as demonstrated by God—frees you from a fear of punishment and allows you to internalize the Law for your own well-being, and consequently, for the well-being of others.

In fact, that's what the Father accomplished in Jesus, after promising centuries before He came,

> The time is coming when I will make a new cov-
> enant with the people of Israel and the people of Ju-
> dah. It will not be like the old covenant that I made
> with their ancestors when I took them by the hand and
> led them out of Egypt. Although I was like a husband
> to them, they did not keep that covenant. The new
> covenant that I will make with the people of Israel
> will be this: I will put my law within them and write
> it on their hearts. I will be their God, and they will be
> my people. (Jer. 31:31-33)

Suppose, on the other hand, that I had simply spanked my son and yelled "No!" when he first wanted to run out into the street. "The law," he would conclude, "exists to placate Dad. I can't trust him to give me the best, namely, the fun of running out to the trucks and cars."

He therefore would decide, "It hurts to get spanked, and I feel alone and afraid when Daddy yells at me and pulls away. So as long as Daddy's around, I'll do what he says."

It sounds good, altogether religious, and even builds up Dad's sense of himself as a firm and strong enforcer of good behavior. But the unsettling question otherwise hidden in that reasoning, awaits both voice and action: "But when Daddy's *not* around....."

Fast forward to teenager, and you've got trouble, big time.

As with ancient Israel, the Law is in the Book, but not in his heart.

OBEDIENCE WITHOUT TRUST

Via punishment, the boy learns obedience, but not trust; law, but not relationship.

If you keep the law not for your own good, but just for your father's approval, you can discount the law if you can discredit your father. Since every dad is a sinner, sooner or later that won't be hard for any son to do. In order to disobey Father God, even Adam needed only the Snake's rationalization that God is a jealous egomaniac. Similarly, my generation of young men in the sixties convicted our fathers of racism, militarism, and sexism—and promptly leapt into self-destructive rebellion.

The law, therefore, prompts rebellion precisely insofar as it short-circuits relationship. The Law can confer rank, but only the Spirit can confer sonship (see Rom. 8:14-16).

The Israelites in Jeremiah's time lacked heartfelt relationship with the Father, and so they couldn't discern His loving intent. Like Adam, they readily believed the snake's lie that the Father was withholding the best from them. "How come the pagans get to have all the fun?" they essentially complained. Thus groaning under the Law, they "did not keep that covenant," but succumbed, rather, to the seductive pleasures of their pagan neighbors (see Jer. 2:23-25).

Without relationship with the father, exhortations to and enforcement of "moral behavior" only foster shame, which beckons rebellion.

What happens when Dad has laid down the law but is not present to enforce it—for example, when the boy is running out with all the others after play group? Clearly, he's free at last to do what he thinks is best for him—and heads right for the street.

Some time after his curbside warning cries, my son and I were driving home from a city playground along a busy, four-lane thoroughfare. As we passed through a particularly run-down section of town, I was shocked suddenly to see a little boy, about two, teetering on the curb just a few feet from cars speeding by.

"Oh, no!" I exclaimed. "Look at that little boy, about to walk right out into the street!" Heart pounding, I asked Jesus to protect the boy as I signaled quickly and lurched around the next corner, stopping quickly by the red curb where I could see my son at his window.

"Where's the little boy, Daddy?" he asked. "Where are we going?"

"The little boy is playing back there, too near the street," I said, pointing down the sidewalk and leaping out of the car. "It's very dangerous for him, and Daddy needs to go help him. You'll stay here by yourself for just a little bit and I'll be right there where you can see me. Pray and ask Jesus to protect the little boy. I'll be back in a minute."

Strapped in his car seat, he nodded matter-of-factly as I shut the car door and dashed off down the sidewalk.

To my relief, the boy had stepped back from the curb but was still walking aimlessly in the grass between the curb and sidewalk. He didn't respond to my questions in toddler-ese, but I managed to get him to go across the sidewalk and sit beside the apartment building where he likely lived. Spotting a pay phone across the street, I ran to call the police.

When an officer had been dispatched, I raced back to my son and drove back toward the apartment building driveway to watch the boy and wait.

"Is the little boy OK?" he asked immediately, as I jumped in the car.

"Yes," I said, pulling quickly out into traffic. "The boy is OK. I called the police to come and help him." Seconds later, as I entered the apartment driveway and turned to see that the boy was still sitting safely, I noticed that my son was sitting with his brow knit, confused.

WHERE'S HIS DADDY?

And then, with a simple question, he cut through my emergency agenda to the heart of the issue.

"Where's his daddy?" he asked, puzzled.

Where, indeed?

A flush of emotion swept over me as I realized how casually my son assumed every little boy is protected by his father, how deeply he had learned that **relationship with Daddy is the primary issue when danger threatens**.

"I . . . I don't know . . . where his daddy is," I said, swallowing deeply as some primal longing, even profound joy for my son and our relationship together, broke forth. "But the policeman is coming, and he'll be OK."

When the officer soon arrived, I explained to him the situation and then got back into our car. "Thanks for being a good helper and praying for the boy," I said to my son.

A minute later, as the freeway on-ramp opened before us, I glanced into my rear-view mirror and saw my son seated securely behind me. Turning to accelerate, I merged into traffic. And then, I burst into tears, grateful for how the Father had knit my son and me together, and fearful for so many boys—and men—for whom the question Where's his daddy? goes unanswered.

Sure, over the years I've often doubted myself as a father. Did I teach my son correctly about discipline and boundaries? Should I have been tougher on him? Or easier?

These are normal questions that all dads I know ask. But often, the only credible answer lies in trusting that I did the best I knew how at the time. Hopefully, I'm learning and growing. That means I'll be a better dad this week than I was last week.

Still, I wasn't as good a dad last week. That means I need grace from "the Father from whom all fatherhood in heaven and on earth receives its name" (Ephes. 3:14NIV footnote).

Thank God, I've got it.

7

Brushing up on Fathering[6]
Imitators of the Father

Be imitators of God, therefore, as dearly loved children. (Ephes. 5:1NIV)

THE SMALL, KID-SIZED BRUSH and colorful dinosaur-labeled toothpaste lay ready on the bathroom countertop. Deliberately, I knelt before my almost-three-year-old son for The Lesson. It had been a long day at work with plenty of frustration, but I was determined to do my fatherly best and get this job done.

Smiling broadly, I reached out and patted the boy on his shoulder. Engagingly, he smiled back, and a neat row of four tiny white teeth beckoned from his top gums.

"Now, we haven't brushed your teeth before," I began evenly, "but tonight Daddy's going to show you how to do it." Positioning his shoulder against the countertop, I reached for the brush and paste. "First, we put some yummy tooth paste on the brush," I noted, forcing a smile, "and then we're ready!"

Squeezing a dab of paste, I reached for his chin. "Now, all we have to do is open your mouth..."

Curious, the boy yielded as I pushed his mouth open.

"Now, I'm going to put the yummy paste on your teeth and make them all clean!" I proclaimed. "Open up for Daddy!" With my thumb tucked into his mouth, I set the brush against the boy's teeth and pushed on it.

"Yaahhh!" he screamed immediately, biting my thumb and jerking back from the brush. "No, Daddy!" he shouted, white streaks of paste-spit dribbling down his chin. "No! No!"

Kids' teeth, I discovered, may be small, but they're not dull. Smarting, I shook my hand and then seized his shoulder. "Now look, this doesn't hurt, and it's good for you!" I barked.

Catching myself, I took a deep breath and spoke evenly again. "Just do what I tell you, and it'll be over before you know it. Now open up again!" Deliberately, I thrust the brush toward his mouth—and once again, he leapt back.

"No brush!" he spat out, spraying paste and saliva. "No! No! No!"

NO PLAN B

In that moment, animated visions arose in my mind, the gist of which declared that my Good Fathering award would have to wait.

Grasping after self-control, I sighed again and hesitated.

I had no plan B.

Teaching a boy to brush his teeth hadn't seemed that complex. Yet the throbbing in my thumb belied that hope—even as, standing there before me drooling white with spit, **my little son stood as an angry monument to my defeat.**

Reluctantly, I reached for a nearby washcloth, wiped his face, and stood up. Placing his toothbrush back on the countertop, I shook my head, uncertain.

I was tired, and suddenly, it seemed awfully late. "OK, the lesson's over," I declared at last, heaving a sigh. "In fact, we're all going to bed."

Ashamed of my over-reaction, I turned away. As much for distraction as hygiene, I grabbed my own toothbrush from the rack beside. Moments later, as I whipped a rabid froth onto my teeth, I glanced down into the mirror.

There, to my surprise, a startling scene was unfolding. Three feet below my bicuspids, a little boy was stretching to reach for his toothbrush high above him on the countertop. Looking up and watching intently, his eyes laser-locked on my hand, he pushed the brush toward his face.

Transfixed, I watched, brush-in-hand. Scouring his ear as much as his mouth, the boy nevertheless fixed his gaze on me as he smeared lips, chin, cheek, and ear white with paste.

I dropped to my knees in front of him, amazed. Wiping my face quickly with the back of my hand, I met his eyes.

"Yes...yes," I spoke quietly, brightly. "That's it...you're getting it...just aim it more toward your mouth." I lifted my own brush to my mouth. "Like this."

And to my amazement, he did it.

Like that.

Like me.

Puzzled, yet determined, I leaned closer and opened my mouth. "Shee?" I slurred, laying the brush on my front teeth and pushing.

The boy did see. In fact, to the very best of his ability, he did exactly what he saw me doing.

After a few minutes, his white-plastered face beaming with self-satisfaction, the boy stood smiling, a monument now to...to what?

Conflicting thoughts warred in my head. My son had disobeyed me, said No to me. Shouldn't I punish him for that? And yet, if the task were truly to teach him to brush his teeth, that had been accomplished. Even cheerfully.

Still looking at me, the boy waited.

JUST LIKE DAD

"Son...," I began hesitantly, "you...you really *want* to brush your teeth, don't you? I mean, you saw me doing it...and then you wanted to do it, too..." Drawn by the mystery, I paused as it hit me. "Just... like me...."

Puzzled now, the boy looked at me as if to say, "Hello? What planet do you come from? Of course I want to do it like you—you're my father, and I'm your son!"

It's so simple.

But why so hard to grasp?

As I prayed later, I sensed God was showing me His larger plan for a father and son: He has ordained the father to confirm manhood in the boy, and placed within the boy a longing to receive it. **Part of Dad's job, therefore, is to present so winsome a model of masculinity that the boy's longing after manhood is affirmed in his heart by what he sees in Dad.**

"Yes," his budding masculine soul cries out, "I want to be like that man!" And because in a profound, even organic sense he is indeed like his father, the "lesson" of manhood strikes home.

How many men, however, grow up believing from experience with Dad that a father's job is to force his son to do the right thing? And then, either as sons or as dads ourselves, we discover that it just doesn't work. It doesn't produce real men, but either passive conformists or aggressive rebels.

It's good to want your son to do the right thing, to become the man God has called him to be. But the Toothbrush Lesson convinced me **to re-examine my role in helping him get there.**

And my motives as well. In fact, my great frustration with The Lesson grew largely out of a sense that I'd failed in my duty as a father, and therefore felt ashamed. My son was not cooperating with my desire to succeed—no matter how nobly focused. In that sense, he was refusing to bear my shame.

Insofar as a dad realizes his inadequacy but doesn't take its shame to Jesus, who alone can bear it, he'll try to cover it himself. **The simplest way to keep a boy from seeing your shame is to dump it on him**—that is, to intimidate and overwhelm him with your own power, so he feels like the weak, inadequate guy himself and is afraid to note your brokenness.

This is the root of shame-based religion, with which unfathered leaders cover their shame by exhorting other to impossible standards of behavior.

In this painful charade, nobody goes to Jesus—and nobody learns to trust either Dad or their own ability to succeed.

As sons, may we forgive our fathers.

As fathers, may our sons forgive us.

8

Pre-School Hugs
Sex Ed 101 for Dad

What the Father does, the Son also does.
(John 5:19)

IN THE OLD DAYS, WE CALLED IT "the birds and the bees." I don't know what they call it today, but no matter—the stirring when boy meets girl hasn't changed.

What *has* changed, however, is that I'm now the father. When my son was born, in fact, I just assumed that I could cruise for at least 12 years before we'd ever have to deal with girls.

Not.

In fact, a surprising phone call from the pre-school principal upended my fantasy.

"Mr. Dalbey," she began deliberately, her measured tone setting me on shame-alert, "we need to discuss something about your son."

I had just returned from a week-long ministry trip the day before, and wasn't ready for this. *Oh, no!* I thought. *Not already! A call from the pre-school principal?* As my inner shields went up, I strove for a casual response. "Uh, well, sure. What did you…want to talk about?"

"Well, it's about the way he's been acting around the girls at school."

"The girls?" I blurted out incredulously, blowing my façade. "I mean, well, of course he's only three years old, so what could possibly be the problem?"

ROUGH WITH GIRLS

"Actually," the principal allowed, hesitating, "we're not exactly sure. All we know is that he's been getting a little rough with the girls. He's not that way with the boys."

I couldn't believe it. He was such a well-intentioned boy. Passionate, lively, and engaging, sure. But not mean or violent. "You mean, he's hitting the girls or something like that?" I asked.

"No, no—nothing like that," she assured. "He's such a pleasure to have around, and that's why we're confused. The problem seems to be when he comes to school and goes to greet other children at the beginning of the day. He says hello to the boys, but when he sees a girl, he runs up and puts his arms around her—as he did this morning.

"We encourage children to hug each other, but this is different. He clearly doesn't mean any harm, but he tries to pick her up and gets rough sometimes—enough to throw them both off-balance and they could fall down. We just don't want anyone to get hurt."

My shame eased, and I sat back quietly, baffled. *Now, why in the world would he do something crazy like picking up girls and being so rough?*

"Well, thank you very much for letting me know about this," I offered. "My wife and I will talk it over and see that it doesn't happen again."

Later, Mary and I sat together, puzzling over the principal's call. *Where*, we wondered, *did he ever see such rough behavior toward girls?*

We didn't have a television, precisely because we didn't want him to see such negative images and model after them. Nowhere among our friends or in any family experience could we remember his seeing anyone treat a woman roughly like that.

"He was so happy to see me at the airport yesterday!" I declared to Mary, exasperated as jet lag from my trip began to take its toll. "He hasn't left my side since. I don't get it. We've had such a great sense of bonding together and he's been so happy. It doesn't make sense. I mean, he's never seen me do anything like grab a girl and pick her up like what the principal described, much less throw her down!"

Suddenly, Mary and I looked at each other and froze.

"The airport!" I exclaimed. "Yes, of course—that's it! That's the way I hugged you!"

I had been excited to see Mary again, and rushed off the plane to the gate. When I saw her and my son standing together, I ran up and put my arms around her, picked her up, and shook her in joy!

And the boy was watching.

In fact, when I set his mom down and turned to pick him up, his face was beaming. I had assumed that his happiness came simply from seeing his daddy again. But now I saw another source of his delight. **The boy was seeing the man's joy in holding the woman, and his masculinity bonded with that vision, determined to experience it in his own life.**

Clearly, pre-school was his own place to greet a girl—just like Daddy at the airport!

Together, Mary and I smiled at last and shook our heads in amazement.

"Like father, like son!" Mary laughed.

BOUNDARIES WITHOUT SHAME

"Amen," I sighed—pleased that my son was modeling after me, but thinking ahead, wondering how I was going to curb the boy's good and natural expression without shaming him.

That afternoon I picked him up after pre-school, and when we arrived home, I followed him into his room. We sat on the floor and played with his wooden trains awhile, and then, with a deep breath and a prayer, I began.

"I'm glad I'm home again from my trip with you and Mommy," I said.

"Me, too," he nodded, reaching for the locomotive with the blue wheels, his favorite.

"I'm…I'm always happy to see Mommy and you when we haven't seen each other for awhile," I continued uneasily.

"Mm-hmm," he murmured.

I hesitated as the boy adjusted a line of track. *Lord, help!* I prayed.

"You know, when I'm happy to see Mommy, I like to hug her real tight and pick her up. She likes that a lot."

I put a hand on his shoulder, and he turned to face me. "Daddies like to hug and play with mommies like that," I said. "But it's…well, not really a good idea for boys to do that with the girls at pre-school."

The boy looked at me matter-of-factly, waiting.

"It's fun for you to see the girls at pre-school, isn't it?" I said.

The boy paused, uncertain yet where this was leading. "Uh-huh."

"Well, you can always be happy and say Hi to the girls—and you can give them a little hug Hello and Goodbye. But it's better not to pick her up and stuff like Daddy does with Mommy. Does that sound OK?"

Raising his eyebrows matter-if-factly, the boy nodded. "OK, Daddy," he said.

A moment's pause, and then he reached for the train track. "Do you think I should put two engines on the front like this?" he asked.

I hesitated, then exhaled deeply and smiled. "Yeah—I think two engines would work just great!"

9

Trucks Are for Crashing
Helping Mommy Understand

...his mother said to him, "Son, why have you done this to us? Your father and I have been terribly worried trying to find you."

He answered them, "Why did you have to look for me? Didn't you know that I had to be in my Father's house?" (Luke 2:48,49)

"I BOUGHT HIM SOME NEW TRUCK TOYS to play with!" Mary announced proudly, bursting in the front door from the shopping expedition.

I rose from my desk and stepped out of my office.

"See—I'm learning what boys like!" she declared, beaming. Behind her, a four-year-old smile came bounding, red fire truck in one hand and a bulging toy store bag in the other.

Indeed, she was learning well.

"You got the idea, alright!" I affirmed, hugging her as our son dashed past us into the play room and began setting up a magazine roadway around the coffee table.

"Have fun!" Mary called out brightly to the boy, then kissed me and danced away to her study.

Happy to see the boy absorbed in his trucks and pleased at Mary's success, I went back to my computer.

I left my office door open, and grinned as an energetic range of truck sound effects soon broke out in the play room, from loud Honk! Honk!s to GRRRRrinding downhill gears.

For a moment, the sound of chairs and furniture shuffling interrupted—and then, a symphony of more menacing road crashes exploded, now punctuated with convincing interludes of "BAM! AAUUGH!" and an accompanying "KA-BOOM" thrown in for good measure. Metal against toy metal smashed forth to the whiney tune of an overturned 18-wheeler. Inspired by this chorus of smashings, I returned to my keyboard with renewed vigor.

He really likes those trucks! I thought. *Great background for writing a men's book!*

FEMININE DISCONTENT

Suddenly, another sound intervened, sharp and alien.

"What are you *doing* with those brand new trucks I just bought you?"

At once, I detected the distinct hint of feminine discontent.

"You're going to ruin those nice, new toys. Why are you throwing them against each other like that? Haven't I taught you to take care of your things? Trucks are *not* for crashing!"

Faraway in the land of bearded Vikings, a longhorn bugle sounded.

With a swift click on my Save file, I inhaled deeply.

From the foggy depths of fortitude, Dad arose.

Praying.

You've got to help me on this one, Father! I declared, heading toward the play room. *I'm going to need some serious wisdom here!*

When I reached the playroom door, the scene unfolded. Lines of wooden Thomas the Tank Engine tracks, converted into slides, sloped down from one side of the coffee table and then rose up to the couch. At the bottom of the dip, the fire truck lay on its side, one wheel still spinning as no less than a pickup, dump truck, and school bus lay overturned beside.

Wow—that was some crash! I thought, nodding in approval.

The characters in the scene, however, were not mutually impressed. On his knees, the boy sat puzzled, slightly bent over as a hint of fear beckoned in his eyes. Just inside the door, a woman twice his size stood determinedly, her forefinger poised to make a decisive point.

"Honey," I interrupted quickly, "maybe you and I could just talk this over a bit in the other room?" Then turning to the boy, "Hey, that looks like it was a great crash!"

Exhaling, the boy sat up.

"Go ahead with your trucks," I said. "Just be sure you don't damage the furniture or hurt yourself. Mommy and I will be back in just a minute." Reaching out to Mary, I forced a smile and nudged her toward me as I stepped out of the door.

Come on, Father, lead me through this!

I led Mary into the bedroom, closed the door, and turned to look at her. "I...I want to try to explain something," I began tentatively.

"What's there to explain?" Mary shot back. "I just bought him those brand new trucks hardly an hour ago, and already he's destroying them!"

MORE GOING ON

"Yes, I know it looks like that," I managed, "but actually, there's more going on here than what you might think." Hesitating, I drew in a measured breath as Mary stood confused and angry.

"Listen," I said, taking her hand. "You're such a good mom. You really want the boy to be happy and you bought him those trucks because you knew he'd enjoy them—didn't you?"

"Yes, but—"

"Right," I interrupted. "He really does enjoy those trucks, and I want you to know how much I appreciate your doing that for him— and how you've taught him to take care of his things."

Father, Help! I prayed. *She's really trying hard to be a good mom—and doing great at it. I don't want to sabotage that, but she needs to hear this for the boy's sake.*

"Listen, sweetie," I continued gingerly, "I...I don't know quite how to say this....but you have to trust me that it's really important for a son. Boys...actually, men, too...we see things a little differently than girls and...well, the trucks are a pretty good example."

I took another deep breath, opened my mouth, and....could only shake my head in surrender. Yielding, I lifted my shoulders and spread my hands, palms up. "There's no way to soft-pedal this," I declared. "The fact is, with boys, trucks are for crashing."

Mary drew up with a start, confused. "I don't understand this at all. How could he want to destroy brand new things like that? It's just not right."

"I'm not asking you to understand it," I sighed, smiling thinly. "I'm asking you to accept it.

"Boys just like to see things crash and explode. Maybe it's Freudian, maybe it's just that we like power and action. I don't know how to explain it in any way that a woman can understand.

"What I do know, though, is that when a boy crashes his trucks, he's just doing what boys do. Even big boys. Look at car racing, demolition derbys, all the car crash chase scenes in movies for guys.

JUST BEING A BOY

"He's not being angry or destructive or malicious. He's just being a boy. Please, don't punish him for that. I'm asking you as his mom to let him be a boy and not snuff that excitement out of him. Sure, we can set boundaries, like no damaging furniture or hurting himself or anyone else. But he needs to learn that a woman honors his masculine energy."

Mary's eyebrows went up, her mouth began to open, and quickly, I pressed on. "You don't have to agree with how he expresses it, but you do need to respect him as a boy."

Still confused, but now listening, Mary paused to mull over my lesson.

I hesitated, then decided to go for it. "In fact, I'd really appreciate it—and I'm sure he would too—if you could go back into the play-room now and talk to him. You don't have to lie—just look around at his trucks, and say something like, 'You really enjoy crashing your trucks, don't you?' Maybe you could smile and say, 'I'm glad you're having so much fun.' Then maybe you could give him a a hug or something and go back to your work."

After her harsh words—however well-intentioned as a mom—I knew the boy needed to hear that word of grace directly from her, without me present.

I don't remember exactly what happened after that, except that Mary went back into the playroom and spoke to her son and mine—and soon after she left, the mighty melody of trucks crashing rang out once again.

I honor her for it.

Someday, another woman will, too.

Pleased, I settled into my chair, sighed deeply, and turned back to my men's book. *Thank you, Father!*

Immediately, however, an unsettling thought struck me—and remains to unsettle me even today: What if no man had been present to advocate for the boy and his masculine energy in the face of the woman's anger? Indeed, what would happen to an entire culture if most of its boys had been abandoned by Dad and therefore harbored that fear of women?

10

When the Lion Yawns
Dad as Protector

The Lord your God will lead you, and he will fight for you, just as you saw him do in Egypt and in the desert. You saw how he brought you safely all the way to this place, just as a father would carry his son.
(Deut 1:30,31)

OUR LOCAL, "USER-FRIENDLY" ZOO can be great fun with a first-grader—but his natural squiggly, "do-it-myself" determination kept Dad on edge amid the giraffes and pythons. Every minute, in fact, sparked a fresh outburst of excitement and energetic dashing ahead to see what's next. Worried that he might get lost among the crowds and uncertain what could happen among the animals, I was doing my best to keep up.

The lion exhibit, I knew, featured a large male behind open-air bars only a few feet from a railing and warning sign, "Beware if the male lion turns his back to you"—implying a graphic lesson in how to get marked as lion territory.

Eventually, at a pathway junction between the otters and seals, my son spotted the handy finger-pointing sign, LIONS. "Daddy, look!" he shouted. "Right over here! It's the lions!"

Not content to note the sign, the boy immediately bolted and leapt ahead. As he disappeared dashing around the corner, I broke into a run after him. Turning, through the crowd I saw him racing toward the lion, who lay calmly facing the railing.

Opening my mouth to yell "Stop! Come back to Daddy!" I drew up as, to my surprise, the lion did the job for me. With supreme confidence, this awesome beast decided in that moment to yawn. As steak-knife incisors flashed white from gaping jaws and bushy mane, the little boy stopped dead in fear. Spinning on his heels, he came tearing back to me.

"Daa-dee! Daa-dee!" he cried out, arms uplifted and seizing my hand as he reached me, out of breath.

He insisted on holding my hand the rest of the day, and never again ventured beyond arms' reach of me.

No amount of my exhorting, threatening, or punishing my son could have prompted him to surrender to me so completely. As a father, I say, "Thank you, lion!"

That day, my son began to learn that Dad's boundaries are not simply to buttress Dad's ego, but indeed, to protect himself from harm. In that experience, he internalized those boundaries as his own. For his part, the dad learned that **the art of fathering lies in a delicate balance of establishing safe boundaries while allowing the child a convincing hint of the danger which requires them.**

GRAND PROTECTOR

When your child is very young, as an infant or toddler one of your major roles as a dad is Grand Protector. Quickly, however, you begin to realize that you don't have either the 24/7 energy nor the wisdom to protect your child fully. The frustration in that truth can explode into fierce restrictions. Anger, intimidation, and punishment seem the easiest remedy—but in fact lead quickly to the boy's rebellion and the father's burn-out.

In those years, my job as Dad was to prepare my son for life beyond me, to instill within him values beyond simply my own external, at times confusing orders. Often, my greatest ally in that process was simply this broken world—whose dangers and threats co-opt Dad's most determined warnings.

"Put some gloves on, or you'll get blisters," for example, may be entirely correct and appropriate for Dad to say. But the greatest truth—and the most enduring lesson—comes when the boy scoffs at Dad's warnings, keeps pushing his shovel, and comes away with aching blisters.

Reality trumps rebellion.

Certainly, some realities are too dangerous to allow, and you need to step in forcefully to avoid serious harm. But even these can be occasions for learning.

Once, as a toddler after walking a few months, my son ran barefoot toward the bathroom where I'd just spilled water on the tile floor. "Stop!" I shouted to him. A slight turn of his head showed he heard me, but he chose instead to run defiantly into the bathroom.

I leapt up and raced toward him. Sure enough, his little foot hit the smooth, wet-slick tile and went up in the air. Lunging, I caught his head in my outstretched hand just as he fell backward onto the hard tile floor—banging the back of my hand, but not harming him.

Shaken but unhurt, he burst into tears.

As I picked him up and drew him to me in relief, he paused a second and looked at me through his tears with puzzled astonishment, as if to say, "Unbelievable! Dad, you weren't just yelling at me to promote your own authority—you really wanted to save me from getting hurt!"

INVESTMENT IN DESTINY

Clearly, I could have punished him for disobeying my command. **Yet I wanted him to remember not the shame of his mistake, but the benefit of its instruction.** It was harder for me then, but I considered it an investment in his destiny—and in my own future peace of mind. Even then, I was getting too old to catch desperation forward passes like that!

It seems to me better for a son to learn that he's loved than that he's disobedient. If the touchstone of his identity from Dad is "I'm disobedient," he'll act that out or withdraw in shame. The more he knows he's loved, on the other hand, the more he'll trust and obey Dad—to preserve his own welfare and not just to avoid Dad's anger.

Love focuses on the other's well-being (see 1 Corinth. 13:4-7). It's neither passively tolerant of all behavior in this fallen world, nor aggressively punishing of all mistakes or even of disobedience. Love thrives on a balance of truth and grace—even as "God gave the Law through Moses, but grace and truth came through Jesus Christ" (John 1:17).

Clearly, a loving father-son relationship like that is risky. If you're too graceful, the boy could think you're a wimp and reject your authority altogether. If you're too truthful, he could think you're harsh and feel judged. But when you're out in the middle of the desert, it's just as far back to slavery in Egypt as ahead to the Promised Land. You might as well push on.

"Father, give me wisdom here!" has been my constant prayer as a dad.

Once, as a pre-teen, my son asked if we could rent a particular movie that all his friends said was great. I didn't recognize the title, but we drove to the movie rental store to get it.

There, the promo cover photo featured a man looking into a crystal ball. The back-cover summary touted New Age spirituality, including fortune-telling and divination. With a sigh, I prayed my "wisdom prayer" and turned to my son.

"I know all your friends say this is great," I began, straining for an even tone, "but this is about spiritual things like fortune-telling that are actually dangerous and harmful—not to help you, like Jesus does. The powers behind this do know a few things, but they use that to sucker you into their program and later make you go to them instead of to Jesus for what you need."

Clearly, the boy saw where Dad was going, and became defensive.

"You haven't seen this movie, so how do you know it's bad?" he fumed. **"Everyone I know who's seen it says it's great!"**

Uneasy but determined, I forged ahead. "You're right. I haven't seen the film. But I've read enough on the cover to know what it's about. I don't want you to be exposed to this kind of thing. Your friends are free to see whatever movies they want. But they're not my sons. I'm sorry, but we won't be renting this one."

At that, my son tossed the film box angrily into my hands and stomped out of the store.

WARRING VOICES

It was night time and we were about a mile from our house. He'd never walked alone that far at night, but as he turned away from me, voices warred in my head. "Let him walk home all the way—teach him a lesson!" declared one. "Ah, it's not all that important," offered another. "Go ahead and let him watch the movie."

Unconvinced by either voice, I replaced the movie box on the rack and stepped outside. Looking at the street I saw no boy, but assumed he'd be walking home the way we came.

I got in my car and prayed. *Father, I give up to you. I don't know how to handle this best. I don't want to hurt his feelings and drive a wedge between us, but I don't want to harm his heart with the stuff in this movie, either. Give me wisdom, please! How are you praying for us both?*

I waited awhile—long enough, I confess, to give him time to think about his long walk—and then started driving back home the way we'd come. After awhile, I saw him on the sidewalk and pulled over. *Father, ride with me in this!* I prayed, reached out across the passenger seat, and pushed the door open. "Come on, hop in." I offered.

Pausing, the boy looked at me, considered his options—and got in.

Pulling away from the curb, I eased ahead. "I know you're disappointed we didn't get the video. I'm sure you want to talk about it with your friends who've seen it and it seems unfair that I won't let you watch it."

I sat quietly as the boy turned away from me and stared out the side window. Another sigh, another quiet prayer, and I went on.

"I know it doesn't make sense to you right now, but the spiritual power in that movie will lead you away from Jesus and all he wants for you. You're going to have to trust me on this until you've spent enough time with Jesus to find out for yourself.

"All I can say is, **when I tell you that you can't do something, it's always been just to protect you from how it could harm you**. I want the best for you, and part of my job as your dad is to keep bad stuff away from you. Maybe I'm wrong sometimes on my judgment, but if I think something will hurt you, I'll say No."

A Stop sign came up, and as I braked, I reached out and patted him firmly on the shoulder. "I love you, you know."

Turning to the road ahead, I left it at that. I can only say that our interaction later that evening and afterward seemed unaffected and friendly.

FEW HELPFUL MODELS

Beyond physical protection, I realized from this encounter that I needed to become emotionally sensitive enough to protect my son's heart. This was hard for me, largely because I saw few models of this in my world as a boy. **"Stop crying, or I'll give you something to cry about," was orthodox fathering for my dad's generation—as, of course, for their fathers'.**

Once, when my son was about three or four, a friend of mine visited from out of town with his ten-year-old daughter Janey (not her real name). He quickly began tagging around the house after Janey, who showed a genuine, friendly interest in her pre-school protege. The two enjoyed playing together, and after dinner during dessert, I mentioned that Janey and her father would have to go home after we finished.

Moments later, to everyone's surprise and confusion, the boy began pounding on his plate with a spoon and loudly interrupting the table conversation for no apparent reason. After all polite requests to stop proved fruitless, Mary ordered him off to his bedroom alone, and he ran off defiantly, slamming the door.

As we continued with our table conversation, eventually I could hear a pounding noise coming from my son's bedroom, as if he were hitting the wall. This continued for awhile, until I got so frustrated I decided to go in and show him who's boss.

In the hallway, I managed to get hold of myself enough to ask Jesus for help.

When I opened his door, I was surprised to see him sitting strangely huddled against the wall. Puzzled, I sensed that I was somehow missing the mark.

Father, what's going on here? I prayed quietly, then went in and sat down beside him.

"You're pretty angry, aren't you?" I said finally.

He sat there, stone-faced.

And then it struck me. "Are you sad that Janey's going home?"

He glared at me and snapped "No!"—so angrily that I knew I was on to something.

I began saying over and over to him, "Are you sad that Janey's going home?" He kept saying No, until I thought maybe I'd made a mistake.

And then, suddenly, he broke down and just bawled. "I don't want Janey to go!" he cried out through his tears.

I held him as he cried, and eventually his tears subsided. A few minutes later, we were all back at the table, chatting and laughing. When Janey finally left with her dad, he said good-bye to her at the door with a big smile, turned to the family room and went off to play happily with his trucks.

"I'm worried," I confessed to Mary when he was out of earshot. "Do you think he'll carry that memory around?"

"As long as he can cry, he'll be OK," she said. "It's when he doesn't cry that we need to worry."

11

Reclaiming the Father Instinct[7]
From Jacuzzi to Revelation

> *Remember that the Lord your God....brought you out of (Egypt) with a mighty hand and an out-stretched arm.* (Deut. 5:15 NIV)

"IS THERE A 'FATHER INSTINCT'?"

The men's retreat question-and-answer session had been lively, but suddenly a strange silence settled uneasily over us all. Up to this point, we'd confessed feeling inadequate as dads and how that often makes us pull away from our children in shame. But now, everyone seemed to sense—and not without healthy fear—the quantum leap which this new question promised.

What if we men have an inner resource for fathering, apart from outside models and teaching?

With only one child, then a pre-schooler, I invited any more experienced dads there to stand and respond.

"Well, we've all heard of a 'mother instinct'," one offered hesitantly.

Murmurs, nods, and then, more silence—and puzzled frowns.

Gingerly, I suggested this as a "homework question," and went on with another issue.

Not long afterward, I got my answer in a frightening, but decisive way.

Mary had taken our son to a friend's swimming party, and I was off to a business meeting. I arrived to discover the meeting had been canceled, and decided to seize the opportunity to go visit my son at the party.

As I walked into the pool area—uncomfortable in my dressy street clothes—I saw Mary in the pool helping the boy paddle as he splashed around half-heartedly. When he glanced my way, I smiled and waved at him; immediately his eyes lit up and he began kicking energetically.

Puzzled, Mary turned, and then saw me. **"He sure picked up when he saw Daddy was watching!"** she laughed.

Beaming with fatherly pride, I waved and pulled up a deck chair.

JACUZZI LESSON

Before long, the boy got out of the pool and wanted to show me the nearby jacuzzi. As I knelt beside the edge with Mary, he eased down the steps into the hot tub and onto the foot-wide ledge around the inside, which allowed him to hold onto the tile edge with his head above the water.

I noticed that inside the ledge, the water dropped off maybe another two feet to the bottom, clearly over his head. "Hold onto the edge and keep your head up," I warned in my best firm-but-caring fatherly tone. As he scooted around just beside and slightly below us, I turned to chat with Mary.

Moments later, I was startled mid-sentence as, out of the corner of my eye, I saw my son's head disappear under a swirl of water in the middle of the jacuzzi, his hands reaching out above him as he sank. In a flash, I found myself leaping waist-deep into the Jacuzzi, grasping the boy's arm and yanking him up with me out of the water and onto the cement patio.

As I climbed out of the Jacuzzi and knelt beside him, he wiped his face and smiled sheepishly. "That...was... was fun, Daddy!" he sputtered.

"Well...," I murmured, dazed. Shifting, I felt my shoes squish—and suddenly awoke to what had happened. "Fun?" I shot back, now shaking. "You don't know just how close...."

I stopped as Mary nudged me gently.

"Don't scare him," she whispered.

With a sigh, I realized she was right. Gathering myself, I reached out and affectionately rubbed the boy's soggy hair. "Daddy loves his boy," I said at last. "Can you try to hold on better next time?"

Shaking my head in dismay, I stood up and looked down at my dripping trousers—and suddenly the three of us burst out laughing in comic relief.

Nevertheless, as I drove home soon afterward, both fear and excitement swept over me. *What in the world seized me when I saw my son go under that water?* I wondered. *Where did it come from?*

It wasn't like I saw him go under and thought, "That's my son. He's fallen into water. The water is over his head. He could drown. Therefore, I will leap in and save him." Rather—even like the cry for "Daddy!" a few years earlier—all rational processes had short-circuited. **Something beyond a higher, moral desire to help someone in need, even deeper than animal self-preservation, had activated.**

Almost like...*instinct*!

Even as water from my slacks soaked into the car seat, I straightened up, confident and alert to this new revelation: *I have a father instinct*!

AWED AND TROUBLED

Today, long after plunging into the Jacuzzi after my son, I remain awed—and troubled. What if, in fact, a father instinct is not only a part of manhood, but includes the impulse to save your child from harm?

For openers, the whole focus in the abortion debate would change.

In my ministry, I've been surprised to see many a man emotionally devastated after his child was aborted—even when conception was a fleeting encounter and he had no emotional bond whatsoever to the mother.

Something powerful and mysterious, even spiritual, is going on here. "God made everything," the bible reminds, "and you can no more understand what he does than you understand how new life begins in the womb of a pregnant woman" (Eccles. 11:5).

There's no word in Hebrew for "instinct." In fact, could the "father instinct" be the very Spirit of the Father Himself, akin to when He rescued His "son" Israel from Egypt, as in the above opening Scripture? Could this work of the Spirit stir afresh in a man when his seed sparks life to the woman's egg?

If so, the shallow, self-centered question, Does a woman have the right to determine what happens in her body? would have to yield to the deeper, more compelling one: What happens to a man that allows him to override his father instinct and instead abandon his child, even to be destroyed? And what long-term damage does that do to a man's deepest sense of his masculinity?

My exhilaration gave way to awe: In fact, are there other dimensions of the father instinct—equally unsettling and equally basic to manhood itself—which we haven't yet dared to recognize?

12

Daddy's a Bad Mechanic[8]
(But a Good Son)

I and the Father are one. (John 10:30)

MY DAD NEVER TAUGHT ME much about mechanics. As a man, as a writer, I used to feel ashamed of that—until my three-year-old son led us all to the heart of grace.

A gifted businessman, Dad did, however, teach me how to save money. And there's the rub. My money-saving, do-it-yourself mechanical projects always ended not with a bang but a whimper, at the extra bill for the plumber or tow truck to bail me out.

At 51, I thought I'd learned my lesson. While checking my mail one bright, sunlit Saturday morning, however, I beheld a "special discount" oil-change coupon for "just $25."

"Discount"? I scoffed *Why, I could do it myself for half that!*

OIL CHANGE TIME

A surge of excitement signaled oil-change time for my old VW. When my wife and son left later to go shopping, I began plotting to surprise them—and at last redeem my lost dignity as a mechanic.

For a mere $11.35 plus tax at a local auto supply store, I bought the requisite four quarts of oil and filter, plus a special low-sided drip pan.

No need to buy any special covering to protect my porous, white cement driveway; an old piece of plastic drop cloth from last year's Christmas tree would work fine. Nor would I need to shell out the extra buck for a funnel or storage container; the pan had a special pouring lip, so I could pour the old oil directly into a large, empty bleach jug I'd saved.

Proud of my savings, I sped home confidently and parked on a wide, sloping section of driveway up near the house. Squeezing under the car, I dragged the drip pan on the plastic sheet and positioned it under the oil pan bolt. With a quick twist of my wrench and a self-assured smile, I watched the shiny spout of black oil pour out.

As I unscrewed the filter, a dark splash of oil suddenly spilled onto the drop cloth. *No problem*, I thought. *I'll just wipe it off the plastic later*.

Soon, the bolt and filter were replaced, the new oil poured in—and *voila*! Man and mechanic, merged in victory.

Matter-of-factly, I dragged the drop cloth back out from under the car, now heavy with the full drip pan, and some oil in the pan sloshed over the side. *No problem*, I thought again; *the plastic will...*

And then I saw it.

SEEPING OIL SLICK

To my shock, a thick black splotch of oil was spreading under the plastic, which had torn from my dragging it. As the spill on top flowed toward the edge, I leapt down and lifted the cloth—only to see more oil leaking from another tear.

I knelt there stunned. Holding up the plastic, I gazed in disbelief at the dark oil slick seeping relentlessly across my white concrete driveway.

At that moment, a friendly beep from our van announced that wife and son were home.

Not good, I thought—or at least, to that effect.

Beholding the scene as they pulled into the driveway behind me, my son leapt out of the car. **"Mommy, look!" he shouted excitedly—**

in case the neighbors might not hear. "Daddy thinks he's a mechanic!"

Swiftly, I bundled up the plastic and sopped up the oil as best I could with some paper towels. Rushing behind the fence gate alongside the house, I dumped it all in the trash can—only to remember that it, too, had worn holes in the wheel-less plastic bottom from when I'd dragged it out to the curb on especially heavy trash nights.

As dark oil oozed from below it onto the concrete walkway toward my feet, I recalled a similar scene in a low-budget horror flick, where the monster's blood...

"Daddy, can I help?"

Behind me, my son's voice cut through the panic, and by some compelling and likely gender-related instinct, I saw my chance.

Smiling, I turned around.

With a gracious nod, Mary disappeared into the house.

"Well, sure you can help Daddy!" I declared, turning back with renewed enthusiasm to the drip pan. I set the big empty bleach jug on a few newspapers, this time to be sure and collect any spill. "If you can just hold this jug right here with two hands, I'll pour the dirty oil into it."

Uncertain, but anxious to prove himself to Daddy, the boy grabbed the bleach jug handle gingerly as I lifted the heavy pan.

"All you have to do is just keep it steady in one place," I noted evenly.

Happily, the lip worked. As the oil poured out straight, I sighed in relief.

But redemption was short-lived. The small-mouthed jug, the full pan, shaky three-year-old hands—not to mention anxious dad—collaborated and in seconds, the warm, dirty oil gushed over the boy's hands.

"Yucchh!" he scowled—and let go.

As I lurched to grab the tipping jug with one hand, more oil spilled from the drip pan in my other hand.

"MOMMY!" he broadcast once again to the neighborhood, "Daddy's a BAD mechanic!"

TRUTH HURTS—AND HEALS

The truth, as often said, will set you free. But first—as not often said—it can hurt like wrench-bruised knuckles.

Several days of apologies and much-more-than-$25 professional cement scrubs later, I mentioned the incident in a letter to my parents.

"That's amazing," my mother wrote back. "When I married your father, his mother told me, 'Put tools in his hand and you'll starve. Put a pencil and paper in his hands and he'll make a fine living.'"

I, too, was amazed—and delighted. **Strangely, graciously, those few words of truth from my heritage set me free. In fact, I suddenly felt a distinct, even manly pride in my mechanical bungling.**

I write this story with "a pencil and paper" in my hands. I make a living as a writer.

I'm not a mechanic.

But the good news is, the shame is gone.

I'm a son.

13

Crocodile Hunting with Dad[9]
Your Father's Story Is Your Story

At Mount Sinai the Lord our God made a covenant not only with our fathers, but with all of us who are living today. (Deut. 5:2)

THE THANKSGIVING TURKEY HAD BEGUN TO SETTLE after our extended-family dinner in Phoenix, and amid the chatter of dishes and lively conversation, the women rose from the table to gather in the kitchen. As the half-dozen men drifted outside to the patio, I picked up my pre-schooler son and joined them under a star-speckled desert sky.

There, my brother-in-law host was telling about a bull snake that often visited the patio for shade on hot afternoons. Drawing closer to hear, I felt my son tighten his grasp on my neck and saw his eyes widen—as when I would tell him my own story of crocodile hunting years before in Nigeria as a Peace Corps Volunteer. Among all my stories, that was his favorite and most often requested, relished each time as if it were the first.

COYOTES AND JAVALINAS

Soon, the patio conversation turned to coyotes, then javalinas, the fierce desert pigs. Before long, the voices tapered off and the men fell silent, gazing out together in wonder at the vast desert darkness.

Savoring the moment, I shifted the boy on my hip and smiled. The trip to visit my in-laws had been a spur-of-the-moment plan, and I congratulated myself on taking the leap.

Suddenly, a small but passionate voice burst forth from beside my chest.

"One time, my Daddy and me went crocodile hunting in Nigeria!"

"Wh-what...?" My jaw fell open as I turned to my son's face— brow furrowed intensely, just inches away.

Uncles, brothers-in-law, and cousins looked up in surprise.

"It was very scary," the boy continued, eyes aflame and gesturing sharply with his fists as I stood there holding him. "The rainy time came and the crocodiles came up. After the rainy time stopped, we jumped into the forest to the dry streams to catch him. We put a giant hook on the rope and the bamboo pole and saw his footprints in the sand and went to see if we got him."

Pausing, he shrugged his shoulders, raised his eyebrows matter-of-factly, and lifted empty hands. "But he took the meat and we didn't get the crocodile."

Puzzled and amused, the men looked at each other. "Well," winked an uncle, "you and your daddy had quite a time hunting those crocodiles, didn't you!"

Beaming, the little boy nodded as the others turned to me and laughed good-naturedly.

Shaking my head in wonder, I offered a sheepish grin and hugged my son, hoping the others would forget the embarrassing incident.

Later that night, however, I found myself strangely seized by it and sitting up in bed while Mary slept.

LIE-OR DEEPER TRUTH?

I'd left Nigeria twenty-five years before my son was born. Sure, I'd told him the crocodile-hunting story many times, with plenty of drama. The adventure had thrilled me as a young man, and I could understand why it would be exciting to him.

But how could he tell it to the men as if he'd been right there

with me when it happened? Hadn't I taught my son not to lie?

Overwhelmed by the mystery, I got out of bed and fell on my knees. *Lord, what's going on here?* I prayed. *What have I done wrong that would make my son lie in front of all those men in the family?*

And then it struck me: The boy was dead serious. His intensity was genuine and heartfelt. This was no childish fantasy game. He wasn't lying.

He was testifying.

In that moment, I realized that my son was telling the truth, a deep truth, in fact, that we "modern" men—so unfathered and thereby, unrooted—have forgotten: *The father's story is the son's story.* **What a man has done is his son's history, shaping his heritage, the soil and root from which his seed of manhood grows.**

For better or worse.

In fact, his father's story is a boy's admission ticket to the fellowship of men—as for my son, among his male relatives that desert night on the patio.

I remembered years ago as a boy myself, playing Army with my friends just a few years after WWII. At some point in our play, the question was sure to rise up: "What did your dad do during the war?" Every kid knew that he'd better have a good story to tell, or the other guys wouldn't want you in their platoon.

Years ago, before becoming a dad myself, I used to say that a boy wants to bond with his father. But my son has taught me the greater truth. In fact, a boy *is bonded* to his dad, in both flesh and spirit. The boy needs and longs to affirm the bond that's already there, sculptured like Dad on his very face and rooted in his masculine soul.

ROOTS AND FRUITS

That doesn't mean you're your dad's clone or ancestors reincarnated. Rather, **in order to grow into your destiny, you have to root in your heritage.**

A tree without roots is a tree without fruits.

Granted, confessing the part of your father in yourself is hard for men who feel wounded and abandoned by Dad. Yet, attempting to cut yourself off from the pain of your father's story only traps you—and your son—in it. As an 82-year-old grandfather declared at one of my men's retreats, "Whatever you don't forgive your father for, you'll do to your son."

To forget your father is therefore to forsake not only your past, with both its lessons and triumphs, but your future as well. That's why boys—and men—want so desperately to know Dad.

Some years ago, I visited the Seattle Space Needle, and the tour guide noted that the foundation weights 5850 tons while the Needle structure itself weighs only 3700 tons. **A strong foundation enables a tall structure.**

For some time after my "sidewalk safety" lesson described in Chapter Six, I basked in the glow of seeing how my love had led my son to exercise positive inner restraint. "That's great, Father!" I declared one morning sitting at my desk in prayer soon afterwards. "Now all I have to do is demonstrate my love, and that will protect him from temptations as he grows up!"

Long silence on the other end of the line.

I waited, puzzled—and increasingly worried. And then, I sensed the Father's response:

> *For many years, your love will be enough, even a necessary foundation, and I'm pleased that you are so willing to give it to him. But the time will come when your love will not be enough to deter him from the temptations of the flesh.*

"What…do you mean?" I asked, reeling as my bubble burst. In a flash of fear, it struck me how many years I'd wasted as a young man, running aimlessly from my calling, hurting myself and others.

I fell on my knees. "But Father, I cried, "if my love isn't enough to protect him when he gets older, there must be something I can do then to keep him on track—?"

CONTEST IN BOY'S HEART

Almost immediately, I sensed the response.

> *It is then you shall tell him at last who he is.*

*Tell him the story of my history in him—through you, your father, and your grandfather unto his spiritual ancestors in ancient Israel—**that a love greater than yours might enter the contest in his heart.***

Tell him Who made him, and the kind of men I used, even the history and sin I overcame in them, that he might be prepared for his own calling.

Tell him he's a man of destiny, that my hand is upon him even as his forefathers. Tell him he can deny it, he can hate it, he can run from it, he can pretend he's someone else. But I, his Father, will have my way with him, even as with you, his father. And as I do, he will rejoice and take his destined place at last as my son, even a brother among brothers, a man among men.

I sat quietly for a good while. "OK, Father," I said finally. "I'll do it."

Over the years, I've tried to connect my son both with Father God and with his Dalbey bloodline. I sent him to a Christian grade school, read the bible and prayed with him. I raised him with as little of religion and as much of Jesus as possible.

I've shown him pictures of his great grandfather and great-great-grandfather, telling him what family stories I know. When my father was alive and living on the East Coast, I took him cross-country to be with Grandpa as often as possible.

On one of those trips, when he was 13, we sat at Grandpa's kitchen table one morning, and I asked Dad to speak a blessing over his grandson.

"What do you mean?" Dad asked, intrigued.

"I mean, would you put your hand on the boy's shoulder, look him in the eye, and tell him what you like about him, the good things you hope for him when he grows up as a man?"

I'm both pleased and proud to say that Dad did that wonderfully for my son.

Did all this work? That's not for me to say. I can only say I've done my best to give my son a history and foundation deep enough to grow tall on. I've told him I'll always be here to support and encourage him.

The rest is now between him and the Father of us both.

14

"What Does She Want, Daddy?"
Sex Ed 201 for Dad

There are four things that are too mysterious for me to understand:

An eagle flying in the sky,

A snake moving on a rock,

A ship finding its way over the sea,

And a man and a woman falling in love.
(Proverbs 30:18,19)

A QUICK STOP AT THE BANK TOGETHER and the day's long list of chores would be done. My list, however—as I was soon to discover—did not include the most important task of all.

"Daddy, do we *have* to go to the bank?" The little voice by my side hinted of too much business and too little fun.

"I'm afraid so," I urged, pushing open the heavy glass door and nudging my son inside. "You can't do much without money!"

A long line before a single teller drew me up. My check had to be cashed that day, but this was not exactly a four-year-old's formula for adventure.

"Now, I know this hasn't been much fun," I offered quickly, "but we'll think of something exciting we can do after we finish here."

With a heavy sigh, the boy joined me in the line, drooping his shoulders in disgust and dragging his feet.

Eventually, however, a colorful cardboard stand-up sign in the center of the room announcing "Great Interest Rates" caught his attention, and he ambled over toward it. Drawing close, he put his face near the sign, examined the pictures, and then ran his hand lightly over the surface.

WONDROUSLY SHE CAME

With nothing else to do, the others in line took notice. I was about to call the boy back to me, when suddenly the bright chirp of a little girl's voice broke through the heaviness of our restrained waiting room.

"I just can't wait!" she announced as the door whooshed open.

And then wondrously, in she came, skipping and chattering away to her mommy—a beacon of light and gust of fresh air adorned with curls, colorful red bows, white lace blouse and socks, red skirt and shiny black shoes. The goal-oriented customers in line shifted angrily and glanced at their watches; those more resolved to the moment turned to look and smile.

I looked and smiled, too, then noticed to my surprise that my little son was also looking—and smiling. Indeed, his body language declared that he was no longer simply resolved, but goal-oriented. Immediately, he turned from the colorfully lifeless cardboard to this amazing new creature adorned with vitality and brightness—to say nothing of those dancing curls.

With renewed curiosity and intensity, he drew himself up and moved toward the little girl. Suddenly, he began laughing, stepping, bouncing, skipping. When he drew close, he looked her up and down, bobbed his head from side to side, and gave a tentative hop in the air.

By this time, the drama had drawn the others standing in line. Instinctively, I feared that sooner or later, his innocent delight would lead the boy to touch the girl, but as I made a move to step over and draw him back to me, she saved me the effort.

Stopping in fear before the boy's strange antics, she fell quiet, and then rushed over and grasped her mother's skirt.

Like air rushing out of a punctured balloon, my boy's heart fell depleted. Scowling, shoulders slumped once again, he stood uncertain for a moment. And then, in a flash, he turned and raced over to me.

"Daddy!" he wailed loudly. "What does she want?"

You don't get a chance like this but once in a lifetime.

THAT QUESTION

I reached out and rubbed his head. "Son," I declared loudly, with a nod to our otherwise burdened audience, "we've been asking that question for thousands of years!"

As the line of frustrated and bored bank customers burst out in laughter, I bent down and picked up my son. "It's alright," I reassured him with a squeeze. "You didn't do anything wrong. The little girl looks very pretty doesn't she? Well, she just got a little scared, that's all."

As I held my little son against my chest, the quick thump-thump of his heart knocked on the door of my own heart. *Oh, Father!* I prayed, *Give me wisdom to know how to bless my son as you draw him toward girls. And please, please protect this boy's heart as girls move toward him!*

15

One Ice Cream at a Time[10]
Growing up with the Child's Help

How can you be generous with others if you are stingy with yourself, if you are not willing to enjoy your own wealth? No one is worse off than someone who is stingy with himself; it is a sin that brings its own punishment. (Ecclesiasticus 14:5,6)

THE NEON CONE WINKED in the mid-afternoon sun as my four-year-old son and I strode from the post office with tasks yet undone.

"Daddy, I know something fun we could do!" The little voice rose up brightly from the dark and busy pavement as we marched toward the car. "Let's get an ice cream!"

I hesitated on the hot asphalt as a cool scoop of ice cream leapt into my mind.

Wiping sweat from my brow, I reached quickly for my keys. "No!" I snapped.

Crestfallen, the boy pleaded, his voice breaking. "Why…not, Daddy?"

FATHERLY DISCIPLINES

"Because," I replied—and then stopped, scrolling through my list of fatherly disciplines. He'd just had a hamburger for lunch, nothing on our list had to be done immediately, the bills were paid, and I had the money in my wallet. *Still,* I thought, *you can't just have an ice cream. Not just like that.*

Below me, a small face framed red with dry ketchup looked up sadly, awaiting the word from on high.

I sighed. "Well, OK. You can have an ice cream," I declared,"— later, after you've eaten a good dinner."

"Oh, Daddy, no!" the boy wailed, breaking into tears. "It won't taste as good then. I want an ice cream *now!*"

Again, from across the parking lot, the neon cone waved. *He's got a point,* I thought.

"OK, you can have some ice cream now," I allowed. "You can have *half,* and we'll split it."

"No, Daddy!" he sobbed. "I want my own ice cream!"

Not about to tolerate selfishness, I held my ground. "You can choose the flavor," I barked, "but if you want any ice cream at all, you'll stop fussing!"

With some effort, the boy assessed his options, then drew in his sniffles and quietly took my hand.

MY OWN ICE CREAM

Moments later, we sat silently with a small mound of mint-chip ice cream between us, topped like rabbit ears with two spoons. "You can have your half," I allowed at last.

At once, the boy seized his tool, rammed it into the ice cream and shoveled out a hefty spoonful into his mouth. Quickly, he attacked again. Like exclamation points, creamy white rivulets and pieces of chocolate soon punctuated his chin.

Suddenly, I realized I'd have to eat the other half myself—and fast. If I didn't, he would enjoy the whole thing! I picked up my spoon dutifully and took a taste.

"Hey, that's pretty good!" I blurted out, surprised—and reached for another, larger spoonful that cut without restraint into the boy's side.

That did it.

"DADDY, GET YOUR OWN ICE CREAM!" the boy exploded.

My own ice cream? Startled by the very concept as much as by his outburst, I gazed off beyond the "extra toppings" counter. *A whole scoop, just for me?* I turned back and looked at our cup. *But I haven't yet...*

And then, above the speckled mound of ice cream, I saw him: a little boy, teared and scowling.

From somewhere in the depths of my stomach, a bitterness rose and settled into my mouth.

And then, at last, I knew him.

A lingering hint of mint-chip sweetness beckoned, and I swallowed hard.

"Well, son," I stumbled, "I...I'm sorry. I really am. I mean, you're right. I do want...my own ice cream. I guess it's...it's just hard for me sometimes...to have fun."

Uncertain but determined, I stood up. "I like you," I sighed, smiling at last at my son and reaching to muss his hair affectionately. "Thanks... I mean, for thinking of the ice cream."

Brighter now, the boy smiled. "It's really good, isn't it, Daddy!"

Amazed by grace, I nodded slowly, gratefully. "Yes, son, it really *is* good. In fact, you can go ahead and finish the whole scoop yourself."

And then, with some effort, I smiled and turned to the counter clerk. "I'll have another scoop of mint chip," I proclaimed, "—for myself!"

There in the ice cream store with my little boy, I began to see why Jesus "rebuked" his followers when they tried to turn away the parents who wanted him to bless their children: "Let the children come to me and do not stop them, because the Kingdom of God belongs to such as these" (Luke 18:16).

LAVISH GIFT-GIVING

My little boy has softened my heart—hardened for so long by shame and fear. He's taught me literally to "taste and see that the Lord is good" (Ps. 34:8RSV).

Sure, there's a time to say No to your son and stick by it—primarily when he's doing something that could cause harm. But I sense now that **a boy will heed his father's No only as deeply as he has enjoyed his father's Yes.**

What, indeed, is an uptight dad like me to make of a God who wants us "to enter into the celebration of his lavish gift-giving by the hand of his beloved Son" (Ephes. 1:6TMB)?

Only this: that the Son is the Father's Yes.

At my age, I'm afraid to open up, but I don't have the energy any more to shut down. Who will lead me into this terrifying, promising new life of grace?

Who, indeed, but the child?

Soon after the ice cream incident, I called a friend for help. "I feel trapped," I told him. **"I can't enjoy life, and it's killing me. I don't want it to kill my son.** How do I get free?"

My friend thought for a moment, then answered, "One ice cream at a time."

I wonder: can it be?

I pray: *Father, let it be!*

16

Coyote Moon
The Poetry of Fathering

*This is God's message...: "You can't force these
things. They only come about through my Spirit."*
(Zechariah 4:6TMB)

"I'M READY, DADDY!"

Squinting in the afternoon sun amid the after-school laughter
and shouting, I turned to see my son shifting his backpack onto his
shoulders. Gingerly, I stepped across the parking lot through the crowd
of school kids and bent over, my arms outreached for our usual hug.

"Oh, Gordon!"

I stopped mid-hug and looked back as the principal called out to
me over the din and stepped up beside us.

POETRY CONTEST

Looking down at my son, he lifted his eyebrows and spoke
deliberately. "Don't forget the school poetry contest!" he urged,
then turned to me with a knowing grin. "He's good with words," the
principal declared loudly, so the boy could hear. "I know he's only in
the third grade, but I'm looking forward to reading his entry!"

Below me, the boy lifted his face with a dutiful smile, then lowered it and sighed.

Uncertain but engaged, I shook the principal's hand and thanked him for his encouragement. Turning, I reached down again for my hug—but my son was already walking away from me toward the car.

"So what's the deal with a poetry contest?" I called out excitedly, rushing up from behind.

"Nothing!" the boy scoffed, keeping his face lowered and picking up his pace.

I stepped up beside him. "There's a poetry contest at school?" I pressed. "Hey, that sounds like fun! You heard the principal say you're really good with words—you're going to write a poem, aren't you? I bet you could win it!"

Reaching for the car door, the boy grimaced. "I'm not writing any poem," he huffed, "and you can't make me!"

Whoa—clearly, we struck a nerve! What in the world was his problem? Hey, this was my son—the son of the writer, actually.

And the principal was right. Even though he was only eight, the boy was very good with words. Creative, intuitive, with all the buddings of a writer himself. Even his teacher had said so.

NOT GONNA DO IT

"I...I guess I don't understand," I offered carefully, easing into the driver's seat beside him and straining for an even tone. "I mean, you know how much fun we have thinking of words that rhyme, and I think you could do a great..."

"I'm NOT gonna do it, OK?" the boy snapped.

"You don't have to get so angry about it!" I shot back. "But I'd just like to know, why not?"

Disgustedly, the boy threw his backpack onto the car floor. A frown and misty eyes appeared, then quickly, he turned his face away to the window. "I just don't *want* to!"

I hesitated, then shrugged my shoulders. "Well, I...uh, don't know what's going on. I know you could do a good job writing a poem, but...well, I guess if it's not an assignment, you don't have to if you don't want to."

Lord, help! I prayed as we rode home in heavy silence. *What's going on? You've gifted this boy with great verbal skills and now he doesn't want to use them! Poetry isn't something you can just force out of somebody. If I threatened to punish him and made him write a poem, he'd mess it up, probably even try to!*

Suddenly, a bolt of shame overwhelmed my rationale. *What would the principal say to me when he didn't enter the contest?*

Clueless, indeed powerless, I shook my head in dismay. *OK, Father, I give up. You're the One who gave him this talent, so You're going to have to call it out. I lay it all down to You: the contest, my wanting him to succeed, the principal's disappointment and judgment of me.*

Later at home, as the boy sat reading a book, I thought about checking my e-mails—then decided to make an effort to re-connect.

"Hey, wanna go exploring down at the creek?" I offered.

He paused. To my pleasant surprise, he put down his book. "Sure."

NEW ADVENTURE

And off we went—from asphalt streets and cement sidewalks to grassy field and finally down a dusty path, through the tall grove of sweet-smelling eucalyptus trees.

What adventure, I wondered, *would we find today?* **From coyote bones and coon tracks to Mallard mommy-and-daddy ducks and penny-sized frogs, the creek bed rarely disappointed us.**

Sure enough, a huge culvert drain, big enough for me to stand in, made a great echo chamber, as we threw clickety stones, pirate shouts, and wolf howls into its foreboding darkness. Further along, we were startled to find several dead butterflies, with colorful red and black wings. A quick search of my jacket pockets turned up an old plastic sandwich bag with only a little peanut butter and jelly on the edges—a perfect archeologist's sack for our wing collection!

Later, a large oak tree with knotted rope hanging from a thick branch thirty feet above sent us swinging, Tarzan-style, out over the edge of the creek.

Amid the adventures, I congratulated myself that I really had let go of the poetry contest, and was content just to enjoy the afternoon together.

Eventually, I realized the sun was going down. As I turned to call the boy, I noticed an early full moon perched just above the treetops.

"Look!" I called, waving him up to me. Squatting, I pointed up. "See up there in the sky? We need to start heading home." With a chuckle, I added, "'Cause you know who comes out when it gets dark down here and the moon is out!"

The boy skipped up beside me. "Yeah!" he burst out, eyes wide and scanning the thick brush on nearby slopes. "Coyotes!"

At that, he looked up. "Wow, the moon is glowing—we'd better be going!"

I nodded and stood up to go. And then, it struck me: "Hey, that rhymes!" I blurted out—and caught myself quickly.

"Yeah...!" The boy exclaimed, then nodded hesitantly, his eyebrows lifting as his gaze drifted off. "You're right!"

Together we turned and began walking. And then quietly, the boy slowed and dropped back.

Deliberately—not daring to look behind—I kept up my pace. *Lord,* I prayed, *in case one of us forgot, I took my hands off the poetry contest and laid it all down before you!*

Above us, a pair of birds sang to each other freely and brightly, as ahead, the field path opened. Suddenly, a voice drew up and chirped excitedly beside me.

"Hey Daddy, are you thinking what I'm thinking?"

Very casually, I slowed. "Well, I...I don't know. What're you thinking?"

"The poetry contest!" he exclaimed.

"Oh, yeah, right—the poetry contest," I echoed matter-of-factly. Pausing cautiously, I decided to inch ahead. "Do you think you could... maybe, make a poem?"

TOGETHER BY GRACE

Together on the path, we stopped.

Knitting his brow, the boy glanced away thoughtfully over the glowing treetops, then looked back at me. "How about this?" he offered: "'The moon is glowing/We'd better be going/Soon coyotes will be showing/their faces'?"

Impressed, I nodded. "Hey, that's good! I like it." Hesitating, I nodded again. "Yes—let's hear it one more time."

And hear it we did, many times before we arrived home for dinner. Even during dinner.

In fact, he decided to repeat the first couplet to "make it more scary." Mom liked it, too, and suggested it needed "something to go with 'faces'." We all agreed, and before long the boy added a last line:

> We'd better be going
>
> The moon is glowing,
>
> We'd better be going,
>
> The moon is glowing.
>
> Soon coyotes will be showing
>
> Their faces
>
> In very strange places.

This story has a happy ending. Not just that "Coyote Moon" won first prize in the school poetry contest.

The principal was pleased.

The boy was excited.

The teacher was proud.

And the dad? Well, the dad was humbled.

Because you know, you just can't force what you want out of a boy.

But you can watch for what God is doing in him, and bless it.

And that's the best prize of all.

You win your son.

17

Roots and Fruits
Giving Your Child a History

> *When you have entered the land the Lord your God is giving you as an inheritance..., take some of the first fruits of all that you produce...and put them in a basket...and set it down in front of the altar of the Lord your God. Then you shall declare before the Lord your God: "My father was a wandering Aramean, and he went down into Egypt...."*

(Deut. 26:1-5NIV)

"GUESS WHAT WE LEARNED in school today, Daddy!"

Buckling my seatbelt for the ride home, I smiled and raised my eyebrows engagingly. "Sounds like something exciting!"

"It is!" my third-grade reporter exclaimed. "It's about American history. There was a time in the old days when kids didn't have to go to school!"

My smile froze. No doubt an eternal vacation from school sounded like good news to an eight-year-old boy anxious to get away from the books and ride his bike. My father, however, had told me stories about his own father's boyhood back in the 1880's, before child labor laws—stories that did not include the luxury either of his own bicycle nor the time to ride one.

"So," I began hesitantly, steering us out of the school parking lot. "Do you mean, like, before they had laws saying kids have to go to school?"

"Yeah," the boy nodded, with a sigh of dismay for his own compulsory education. "There weren't any laws at all like that back then."

"Well, yes—that's actually true," I acknowledged. "Sounds like you wish it were true today, huh?"

"Yeah, that would be great!"

READY FOR HISTORY

"Hmm..," I offered tentatively. *Lord*, I prayed under my breath, *is he ready to hear about his great grandfather and the Dalbey men before him?*

Before us, a yellow-vested school crossing guard raised her red STOP sign. As a boy shifted his backpack and stepped out into the crosswalk, I braked thoughtfully.

"Well, those old days were different, alright," I allowed. "So.... what do you think boys did with their time when they weren't in school?"

The boy shrugged. "Oh, I guess they just played with their friends and all."

The crossing guard lowered her sign, and I eased ahead.

"Actually," I ventured, "it wasn't quite like that for your great-grandfather." To my surprise, a lump rose up in my throat. Startled, I glanced away from the boy toward my window, and gathered my breath.

What's going on, Father? I prayed quietly. *Why in the world do I feel like crying all of a sudden? I just want to give my son a history lesson—you know, give him a real-life story to get him more connected to his school work.*

Uneasily, I inhaled deeply and turned back to the road. "You know that I write books, right? I mean, that's why people ask me to speak at conferences and that's how I get money to buy food and things for our family."

Nodding matter-of-factly, my son lifted his brow inquisitively, uncertain where Daddy was headed.

I opened my mouth to speak—and again the lump. And again the deep breath.

"Well...," " I managed, "my...grandfather Richard Dalbey—that's Grampa's dad and your great-grandfather—was born in 1880, about the time your history lesson today talked about. When he was a boy, Richard went to first and second grade, like you. He even went to third grade for a little while, but he left and never finished that year—or ever went back to school again."

With an eye to the road, I glanced at my son. **My bright-eyed, bike-riding-in-the-sunshine, fresh and wonder-filled eight-year-old son.** "When your great-granddad was a boy just about your age," I continued, then paused as the lump rose again, higher and more determined now.

My voice drew up, as if being warned to speak carefully of such holy things. With some effort, I sucked in a breath and exhaled the words, "he had to leave school and go to work in a cloth factory, winding thread by hand around big wooden spools all day long."

Ahead, our street beckoned. Gripping the wheel tightly, I leaned into the turn. "He did that twelve hours a day, six days a week," I said. "He was just a kid. Just a kid...just...like you. He had to leave school in the third grade. Instead of going to school, he went to the factory, early in the morning and stood by a da...doggone machine all day long."

I hesitated as a rush of anger, even rage, rose up in my heart and mingled with unbearable sadness.

Quietness fell upon the two of us, and we drove on. As our house approached, I pulled into the driveway and stopped the car. "The fact is," I said finally, turning to my son, "is that because he couldn't go to school, your great grandpa never learned to read or write."

Beside me, the boy sat uncertain.

This must sound like some science fiction story to him, I thought. *But I guess that's the point. I don't want him to experience anything like that.* In that moment, it struck me: *maybe his great grandfather didn't want him to, either.*

LITTLE BOY'S SHOULDER

"Look….," I began, reaching out to the boy's shoulder. As I touched him, I thought of another little boy's shoulder, moving mechanically hour after hour in a noisy, stinking factory—and lost it.

I cried, then sobbed. I couldn't stop. The pain flooded through my body as I sat there shaking uncontrollably and gripping my son.

Uncertain, the boy sat confused, but attentive.

"I…I'm sorry," I offered finally, gathering myself. "I know this is hard… for you to imagine." I leaned over and hugged my son. "It's hard for me, too. But it's part of where you come from. That's the way it was back then. Country kids worked on the farm and city kids worked in the factories. Only the rich kids got to go to school."

I sat up. "Your great granddad never finished third grade," I repeated, deliberately. "So he never really learned to read. He couldn't read books, newspapers, magazines, anything—even when he grew up."

I hesitated and looked away, trying hopelessly, thankfully, to grasp what that would be like. A deep sense of shame stirred in my gut.

"Can you imagine?" I said finally, shaking my head in disbelief and turning back to my son. "Think of all the books you're reading now in the third grade yourself, and how much fun we have reading together!"

A glimpse of understanding stirred in the boy's eyes.

"But you know what?" I burst out, smiling at last. "Now, a hundred years later, that man's grandson is a writer." Pausing, I lifted my eyebrows and reached out again, this time with a firm pat on the boy's shoulder. "And hey, his great-grandson is a great reader and pretty good with words himself!"

With a remaining trace of uncertainty, the boy smiled.

"Listen," I said. "I want you to enjoy school and playing afterwards. That's what your great-grandfather would have wanted for you—and for me.

"So hey, you don't have to go to school!" I declared.

Puzzled but delighted, the boy sat up, and I gave him a playful jab.

"You get to."

The boy was engaged, but I could see the limits of his tender understanding. Enough had been said; more would need to be told in the future.

STREET CORNER TO COLLEGE

The "more" in my father's story begins in his teens during the Depression, when he managed to graduate from high school—but hung out on street corners with his other unemployed buddies. On one of those street corner nights, "while we were whistling at girls," as he so often recalled, "I heard a voice speak to me—as clear as you speaking to me right now.

"'Go to college', it said."

Through a series of marvelous events, this son of an illiterate steel worker turned to work his way through college—borrowing textbooks from the library, sleeping in dorm lounges, and picking up spare time jobs. "Just when it seemed like there was no way to keep going," he would say with a brightness in his eyes, "somehow something would happen that helped me."

Later, during World War II, he served as a Navy officer on an aircraft carrier and afterwards, earned a Master's in Business Administration.

This is not only who my grandfather and father were; it's who I am. **Even as my son hunted crocodiles with me years before he was born, I sweat out the steel-mill furnace and Nazi submarines.** As I engage my father's story in me, with all its pains and joys, disappointments and promise, I'm rooted in my heritage, assured of my place in this world, and empowered in my destiny.

True, I have no callouses burned into my hands from the steel mill, and I never fought a military battle. But that's the point. Confessing the heritage I bear has positioned me—like my father and his father before him—to give thanks humbly for what my forefathers have given me, to build upon it responsibly in my own time, and to give even more to my son.

Let it be, Father!

18

"I'm Scared, Daddy!

-Are You?"

Remember that I have commanded you to be determined and confident. Do not be afraid or discouraged, for I, the Lord, your God, am with you wherever you go. (Joshua 1:9)

LIKE GIANT SHARK'S TEETH, the jagged Colorado mountain peaks thrust high into the blue sky around us, only to glide slowly by as the chair-lift creaked and whirred overhead. My Norwegian blood notwithstanding, summer is my favorite time at the ski slopes. Nothing beats riding to the top in the sunshine, *sans* slush and chill.

Eight years old, my son sat beside me, gripping the steel waist bar and turning only tentatively to glimpse an occasional downhill mountain biker, bouncing and twisting far below us on the switchback trails.

"Hey," I called out, nudging the boy and pointing to a cloud of dust as one biker fishtailed around a steep corner. "That looks like fun, doesn't it?"

Hesitantly, he nodded, and shifted his grip on the bar.

WHITE CHUTES

As our lift moved over a ravine, on another hillside we spotted two white chutes snaking side-by-side down the steep incline. "What's that?" I asked out loud.

Suddenly, a small sled-sized luge with a rider clinging to side handles shot out from behind a clump of tall spruce pines, zipped down the chute and around a bend. A few seconds later, in the second, parallel chute, another rider flew by.

"Wow!" the boy murmured. "They're pretty fast!"

Indeed they were, and a prayer of thanks arose in my spectator's heart as we rode smoothly and safely, high above it all.

Suddenly, a gust of wind slammed our faces, and blew the boy's hat off. Not daring to release our grip and reach out, we watched as it fluttered awkwardly to the ground, not unlike a wounded bird.

"Well, I guess we can say goodbye to that hat!" I offered quickly, trying to shrug my shoulders.

Rats! I thought, as we swayed high and away. *I just bought that hat and he needs one for sun protection at this high altitude!*

Thin-lipped with frustration, clinging to his chair bar, the boy glanced below and nodded.

A few minutes later, our chair approached the top drop-off spot. As the attendant grabbed hold of it, our seat tilted sharply and we stumbled off onto solid ground at last. Gathering myself, I took a deep breath—and then another in the thin mountain air. Stepping aside for a moment, we stood breathing deeply, thankful at last to feel good old terra firma underfoot.

"Hey, Daddy, look!" my son exclaimed. Animated now, he pointed dead ahead. "That's where the chute rides start, right over there!"

In fact, they did. Right there beyond the stack of tiny white sleds. Too bad we just wouldn't be able to...

"Let's go check it out!" the boy shouted, running past me.

Patting my paid-for, round-trip chairlift tickets in my pocket, I turned to follow—and took a few more extra breaths.

"Wow—Daddy, come look at this!"

As I reached the makeshift booth, the boy was running a hand over the smooth fiberglass edge of a compact, newspaper-sized sled-luge. Two small handles protruded from the sides, and an angled stick in the center broke through the bottom to reveal the rubber tip of a primitive brake. The whole thing didn't look much larger up close than from high above on the chair lift. *Anyone crazy enough to ride such a thing,* I thought, *was out of his...*

"Daddy, wanna do it?"

Sharply, the boy's voice severed my line of thought. I hesitated uneasily, and grasped for an excuse. "Well," I offered quickly, glancing at my watch, "we really don't have a lot of time..."

FASTER WAY DOWN

"Daddy, that's no problem. This would be a lot faster way to get back down than the chair ride!"

He had a point there. Better, we could just jump off the cliff.

"Are you in line for the luge run?"

I turned to see a muff-eared young man and several others waiting behind me, ready to get their tickets and sleds. "Actually, I..." Turning back ahead, I saw my son had already picked up a sled.

"Let's do it, Daddy!" the boy exclaimed.

A few quick breaths and resolutely, I reached for my wallet. Sooner than you can say "life insurance," I had my very own sled and was walking beside my son to the edge of the precipice. There, a college-aged young lady in ski tights her father should know about took my money and led us several steps over to the two chute entrances.

Or exits, depending on your level of confidence.

"Just hold onto the side handles," she noted matter-of-factly, "and pull back on the stick if you need to slow down."

The mighty stick.

Right.

Abruptly, she turned and left us there, alone. As the boy peered over the edge, his eyes widened. I edged over beside him, looked for myself—and took a few more quick breaths.

"Wow....," he whispered, his voice trailing off amazed into the chill air. "That's a long way's down, isn't it, Daddy?"

I glanced over my shoulder and saw the group behind us coming over, sleds-in-hand. "Uh, yes, you're quite right about that, son," I murmured. "Actually, it's pretty steep, too."

The young lady and others were now gathering close behind us, waiting.

And then he said it.

"I'm scared, Daddy!" A second's pause, then louder, he turned toward me as the others began fidgeting impatiently. "Are you scared, too?"

EXPECTANT AUDIENCE

Suddenly the crowd around us morphed into an expectant audience, their impatience suspended, if not frozen in the sting-chill wind.

Father, help! I prayed quietly.

Smiling nervously at my audience, it occurred to me that I might augustly help the boy conquer his fear by firmly commanding him not to be afraid of any danger ahead. In that moment, however, I knew that the fear to be conquered was none other than my own, stirred not by any danger ahead, but by the shame right there in my heart.

Together, we peered over the drop-off. "Well, actually...," I offered, turning to my son and pausing over an extended breath. "Yes. I'm scared too."

There. I said it.

A sigh of relief escaped my lips. With several now-familiar quick breaths, a new strength gathered within me. "But we did see others make it OK. And you know what? We'll do it together, side by side!"

With that, the boy's face brightened. Resolutely, he grasped his sled, stepped to the starting gate, and sat down.

A sideways nod and quick smile to our audience—now chuckling behind us—and I joined my son on the edge of the cliff. "Let's go!" I shouted quickly, lest any second thoughts grasp the mighty stick.

And with a tip of his sled, my son disappeared, literally into thin air.

Holding tightly to my sky-hook "brake," I leaned forward. *OK, Father—let's go!*

As from a catapult, I shot ahead—or rather, down. Sliding wind-whipped, we flew slipping, bouncing, edging precariously up the rim and down the chute, the boy some 10 yards ahead of me all the way.

LESSON IN COURAGE

Hardly a minute later, I rounded the last harrowing bend to see him standing over his sled at the finish line, pumping his fist in victory.

"That was FUN, Daddy!" he shouted, jumping up and down as I yanked my trusty brake handle. To my surprise, it really worked—so well that I tumbled off onto the grassy slope and landed at his feet.

Pulling myself up with a long, deep breath at last, I smacked the grass off my pants and then reached to pat him on the shoulder. "Yes, it WAS fun!" I exclaimed, as together we turned and gazed far up the mountainside at our steep, long-ways-down luge runs.

In fact, it was a lot of fun. More than enough, in fact, to satisfy Dad for a long time.

At once, the boy stirred excitedly. "Let's do it again!" he urged.

With a glance at my watch, I sighed easily and noted in that more hospitable air—not without a hint of relief—that we just didn't have time for another lift-ride to the top.

There was time later, however, to wonder at the conundrum: When I confessed my fear, my son took courage, even delight, in the challenge ahead.

Sure, doing something together with Dad is always good, and we likely would've gone down the chutes together no matter what I'd said to him beforehand. But obviously, something far better had happened. Could it be that the boy was ashamed of his fear, and confessing my own fear had given him permission to be afraid, made it acceptable—and therefore, no longer an obstacle to his accomplishment and enjoyment?

In fact, could this reflect the heart of a Father God who sends His Son to endure the worst of physical pain, so that we need not fear obstacles to our destiny, knowing that He's with us in any suffering that entails?

Questions remain. Meanwhile, on the windy mountain slope that day I learned that **a father can impart courage and strength by standing with his son in fear and weakness.**

Like grace, it makes no sense.

But like grace, it makes a man.

19

Not like Chicken Eggs
Sex Ed 301 for Dad

Then Adam had intercourse with his wife,
and she became pregnant. (Gen.4:1)

OUR SON'S FIFTH-GRADE TEACHER at his small Christian school had been called out of town for a day and asked Mary if she would substitute for her. Uneasy but determined, Mary agreed.

We knew all the kids were well-behaved, and I expected a great report on the class work when Mary got home.

What I didn't expect was the report on female biology.

Later that afternoon, my son burst into the living room with typical after-school energy, tossed his book bag down by the door and ran out to his trampoline. A minute later, Mary walked in, shaking her head amazed.

"How'd it go with the kids?" I asked cheerfully.

"The kids were great," she acknowledged, then cut sharply to the chase. **"But you need to talk to him right away!"**

"Talk to him?" I asked. "About what?"

"About girls!" she declared.

"'Girls'?" I echoed, confused.

TIME FOR THE TALK

"Yes, about girls. Listen, there are girls in his class now with breasts. I just didn't realize girls matured so fast these days."

"Well," I offered gingerly, "I…I mean, actually, neither did I."

"You've got to tell him now about periods and everything," Mary declared quickly, her inner Registered Nurse melding urgently with her Ph.D. in psychology. "Girls in his class are going to begin having periods soon if they haven't begun already. One of them could have an accident, and I don't want him to be scared by that."

Puzzled, I forced a smile. "An 'accident'?"

"Yes," Mary declared. "The girl could begin her period sitting right at her desk or something and not be prepared. If he saw her bleeding at her desk, it could be upsetting for him."

Not only for an eleven-year-old guy! I thought. Suppressing a grimace, I took a deep breath. "Well, sure, that would, uh, yeah… certainly be…unsettling. No problem, we'll…, I mean, I'll get right on it."

"You've got to do it soon," Mary urged.

"Yes, sure, soon," I promised. "Don't worry—I'll take care of it."

With that Mary turned and left, again shaking her head in dismay.

Father! I cried out quietly. *How am I going to take care of this? What am I going to say? How much does he know already? He's hardly 11 years old. Sure, I had crushes on a girl or two when I was that age—but do we really need to go there yet?*

Suddenly, the word "accident" popped into my mind. With another grimace, I determined to plunge ahead.

For openers, I knew this would have to happen away from Mommy, even from the house. Later, when his after-school snacks had settled in, I suggested to my son that we hike to a fallen tree maybe half a mile from our home, our ground-level tree fort.

GIVE ME WISDOM

He agreed, and as we walked along and chatted, I searched for a good way to approach all this. *Father*, I prayed, *give me wisdom here.*

I want to deal straight up about sexual stuff with him, but I don't want to go beyond where he is at this stage and what he can understand.

Eventually, we approached the fallen pine tree, dropped to our knees and crawled into our "secret hiding place" within its branches. Whisking away some pine cones, I sat down and gestured for the boy to sit opposite me.

"Mommy said it was a good day at school," I began tentatively. "How was it having her as your teacher?"

The boy nodded. "It was OK."

"Uh huh," I offered, stalling for time. I prayed again quickly, but had no sense of how to proceed. I decided to begin at the beginning, and talk first about conception.

"I wanted to talk about a few special things today," I began. **"Mostly about boys and girls, and how babies are made."** Pausing, I received his nod, and pressed on.

Suddenly, our cat Coco came to mind, and that seemed a good place to start. With two males in the family already, Mary had insisted on a female pet to balance the hormonal scales.

"You know Coco is a girl," I noted, "—and a mammal."

"Yeah," the boy nodded, curious about where all this was going. "I know that."

"Now girl mammals all have something called ovaries sort of below their belly button on both sides—like the word 'oval,' the shape of an egg—and that's where they make eggs."

His brow furrowed.

"Not like chicken eggs!" I blurted out, leaping to clarify. "I mean, they don't have hard shells or anything like that."

Come on, Father! I begged, scrambling for dignity. *I'm halfway out into the river now. You've got to get me to the other side!*

MAMMAL EGGS

Hastily, I pressed on. "Mammal eggs are really small, pretty much microscopic, and girls keep them in their ovaries. When a female mammal begins to grow up, like the girls in your class now, every so many weeks, an egg comes out of her ovary. For human beings, a woman lets out an egg every 28 days—about once a month. It's like the same time as when the moon comes and goes. In girls, all this usually starts when she's about 11 or 12 years old. One sign is the girl starts to grow breasts, which of course are for a baby to get milk from."

I paused and smiled. "I doubt you remember it, but you got plenty of milk from Mommy like that when you were really little!"

Managing a smile, the boy shrugged his shoulders.

"Now, men don't have eggs," I continued. "We have what's called 'sperm,' which we make in our testicles—the two round things in that sack just below your penis. Sperm are not exactly oval, but more like real small tadpoles with a tail, and they kind of swim along, though you can only see them in a microscope too, like the egg. You can't get a baby with just the woman's egg. There has to be a man's sperm to swim to and go inside the egg. That's called "fertilization," and that's what makes everything start to grow into a baby."

The boy nodded, intrigued.

More comfortable now, I pressed on. "So when a woman's ovary makes an egg, it moves from there down a tube to her womb, which is like a sac near her stomach that goes down and opens out at her vagina. The womb is where the baby grows until it's ready to come out and be born.

"When the egg comes down there from the ovary, it sticks to the edge of the womb and begins to connect to the mother's blood vessels. If it's fertilized with a man's sperm, it eventually sticks and holds on there for good, so the baby can get the food it needs from the mother's blood.

"If there's no sperm there and it's not fertilized...," I hesitated for a nanosecond, and decided to leave it at that—"after awhile it kind of tears away from the edge of the womb. That makes the woman bleed, which goes on for a few days. Those days are called a 'period,' or 'menstruation'—like the Latin word *mens* for 'month'—remember the 28 days and the moon cycle?"

"Yeah," he replied, with a trace of genuine interest.

"Anyhow, the blood from the tear comes down her womb and out her vagina, and so women put some padding there—sometimes called a Tampax or Kotex—to soak it up so it doesn't make a mess.

"A woman can figure out when all this is going to happen—like I said, about every 28 days. So if it doesn't happen, if she doesn't menstruate or have a period and bleed, that means the egg is stuck on inside for good because it's been fertilized, and the baby will begin growing in her womb."

At that, an embarrassing memory came to mind. I prayed quickly, and sensed a green light to go for it.

"When a girl is having her period," I noted, "she usually can't go swimming, because the blood might come out in the water and embarrass her. No one ever taught me these things, and when I was a little older than you in high school, that caused me to wound my girlfriend badly.

"One day, a friend with a swimming pool at his house threw a pool party and my girlfriend and I went. About 20 of us kids were there. When I and everyone else had our bathing suits on and were beginning to jump in the water, I noticed my girlfriend hadn't changed and was still in her regular clothes. It was a small area around the pool and everyone was kind of crowded in and chattering together.

"'How come you haven't got your swimsuit on?' I said out loud to her. Everyone else heard me, and she blushed and murmured something like, 'I'm not going swimming.'

"'Well, why not?' I asked loudly, confused.

"'I just…don't want to,' she managed.

The rest of our friends heard me, and kind of turned away from me in embarrassment. Everyone else knew my girlfriend must be having her period, but I didn't know what was going on. My ignorance shamed her in front of all our friends. I don't want that kind of thing to happen to you—or to your girlfriend."

A LITTLE CRANKY

I paused. *Anything else, Father?* I prayed.

"Oh yes, one more thing" I added. "You can probably imagine that all this is not much fun for a woman, so she tends to get a little cranky while it's going on. **Just remember: It's not your fault.**"

The boy nodded—and with that, we sat quietly.

"Anything you wonder about or want to ask me about all this, with girls and all?" I asked finally.

He shrugged slightly. "Not really."

Are we done, Father?

"But we need to put a few branches over the tunnel where we come into the fort," the boy added matter-of-factly.

"Right," I nodded, exhaling deeply with a smile. "We don't want anybody to find our secret place!"

Later, we crawled out of our tree-cave, gathered some brush, and covered the entrance with it—almost like coming out of a womb, born again as men together.

The hike home seemed a lot easier than when we first set out, and I entered the house with a lively step. As my newly educated son took off to play in his room, Mary came out quickly.

"How did it go?" she asked, eyes narrowed and intent.

"Pretty good, I think."

"Did you talk to him about periods and all?"

I nodded confidently. "You bet."

"What did you say?"

"I told him everything. Menstruation, eggs, sperm, the works."

"Well….OK," Mary allowed. "Anything else?"

"Actually, yes—just one more thing," I noted. "I told him that when it's going on, girls tend to get cranky."

Mary's eyes widened. "You said *what*?"

"Hey, you asked me to tell him the whole story!" I laughed, reaching out to hug her.

As I embraced my beloved Ambassador of the Mystery, I let out a sigh of relief at last. There would be more to talk about later, I knew. Still, I had a distinct sense in that moment that my Father God had His hand on my shoulder—and was pleased.

20

The One-Minute Father
Mercy Triumphs over Judgment
(James 2:13)

TRUE OR FALSE: The best way to change other people for the better is to show them their mistakes.

Put it another way: If you just point out clearly and forcefully enough what someone is doing wrong, the person will change and do it right.

Most of us know from painful experience that's false. And yet too often, we act as if it's true. **In fact, I don't know another human belief held so deeply that fails so often and so miserably.**

Could it be, rather, that we human beings change most deeply and positively when we're loved, appreciated, and encouraged?

CONVERTED TO MERCY

Some years ago, I was converted from judgment to mercy by Davie (not his real name), an 8-year-old boy I agreed to mentor a few years after his alcoholic father had died of a drug overdose.

Through an arrangement with Davie's mother, I'd seen him one afternoon a week for over a year. Though we spent most of that time having fun—playing ball, flying model planes, and such—eventually I became concerned to see him sloughing his schoolwork and drifting toward a rougher bunch of boys in the neighborhood. I was wondering how to approach him about it, when early one evening I received a frantic phone call from his mother.

"The school called and said Davie skipped class again and didn't do his math," she declared, frustrated. **"I've done everything I know how--please come over and see if you can do something!"**

Sighing uneasily, I agreed to try.

As soon as I arrived at the house, Davie's mother met me at the doorway shaking her head in dismay. "He's in there," she said, gesturing toward the kitchen. Thank you for coming—I need to leave and pull myself together!"

Alone, I hesitated, then stepped into the house and headed for the kitchen.

The boy was sitting at the table, head propped up on his elbow and looking away, his math book and papers scattered about him.

"Uh...Hi, Davie," I offered. "How about we go and maybe...uh... take a drive together?"

Davie sat unmoved. And then with a disgusted grunt, he rose up without looking at me, dropped his pencil emphatically, and walked past me out to the car.

As we drove off, the boy deliberately turned his head away from me and gripped the door handle. Uncertain but dutiful, I began telling him that he was messing up his future, that he had to stop cutting school and begin doing his homework. As he sat quietly, I ran down his mother's list of all his bad behavior from the week before.

To my frustration, Davie just clammed up and looked out the other window. In fact, he grew more tense and distant every time I tried to tell him something else he'd done wrong. As my anger grew, by grace I thought to pray quietly. *Lord Jesus, help! I'm not getting anywhere with Davie. How do I get him to start doing things right?*

WHAT YOU LIKE ABOUT HIM

As the beach drive came into view, a strange thought occurred to me: *Tell him what you like about him.*

Puzzled, I balked. Frankly, I really didn't like a whole lot about Davie at that point. Yet it struck me that he already knew what he'd done wrong. I wasn't telling him anything new. What he didn't know—and what would be genuinely new—was what he'd done right, or what I liked about him.

As the young boy clung to the door across from me, I surrendered. *Father,* I prayed, *help me think of good things to say to him!* Soon, I remembered when I'd given him a pack of chewing gum and he'd shared several sticks with friends. Desperate to try anything, I plunged ahead.

"Do you know what I like about you, Davie?"

Surprised, he turned away from his window to look at me, knit his brow, and then turned back away.

I pressed on. "You're generous and share with your friends—like you did with that pack of gum last week. I like that about you."

Come on, Father—I need more things to say! Before long, other things came to mind, and I began just speaking them out one by one to the back of Davie's head. Somewhere after the third good thing, Davie finally turned to face me—and listened intently through the rest of this new and positive list of his actions.

When after five examples I could think of nothing more to add, the boy sat quietly—not angry any more, but looking confused. Uncertain myself what was happening—*was he really hearing me, or just pretending?*— I pulled over to the curb.

"I know what I've been saying sounds sort of new to you," I offered.

Unsure, I prayed under my breath, *Father, help! Where do we go from here?* As I looked at Davie's face, knotted strangely in confusion, suddenly it struck me: *He's not hearing me!*

At that, an altogether basic, simple idea came to me. "Davie," I said, "help me out a bit here. Would you mind please just repeating what you heard me say—you know, the five things I like about you?"

Then came the shock.

Davie looked at me, wrinkled his brow, then dropped his eyes. "I...I don't remember," he murmured wistfully.

USED TO DOING WRONG

I sat stunned. **Here was a little boy so used to being told what he'd done wrong, that he couldn't hold onto anything I told him that he'd done right.** Something in my heart moved, and I swallowed hard. Gathering myself, I spoke again.

"Listen, Davie," I began, "I'm sorry that I just dumped more bad news on you today. You don't need that from anyone else."

Reaching out, I held his shoulder firmly. "I really want you to hear what I'm saying to you," I declared. "So I'm going to say it one more time, and I want you to listen closely, OK?"

Uncertain, Davie glued his eyes to mine. Then slowly, I repeated my list of the five things I like about him.

When finally I stopped, the boy sat eagerly, like a puppy awaiting a bone. "Do you think you can tell me now what I like about you?" I asked.

Without hesitation, Davie leapt forward and quickly named all five—almost word for word!

"That's great!" I exclaimed, patting him on the shoulder. Before long, we were both talking excitedly about the good things I'd seen him do and how much I liked him.

Eventually, I noted that we needed to get back home. When we walked in his house, he went straight to the kitchen, sat down and gathered his papers. Soon, he was doing his math problems one-two-three as I sat beside him.

When he had finished his homework, he turned to me with a self-satisfied grin. "Got some more?" he asked.

Amazed by grace. I gave him a few more problems, and then had to leave.

Later, it struck me: Could this be this how God sees us?

Our biggest problem is not that we don't know what we've done wrong, but that we just can't stop doing it (see Romans 7:14-8:1). That is, we're so paralyzed by condemnation that we can't allow the Father to save us from the effects of our sin.

Some years ago, the bestseller list included a small, 60-page book titled *The One-Minute Manager*. Its entire message could be summed up in a single sentence of advice: Sneak around your office, catch employees in the act of doing something right, and tell them.

Its shock value lay in its embarrassing simplicity.

As a Christian, I had to wonder: Why is this such radical, best-selling news to a society filled with churches?

POWER IN AFFIRMING

Because we have forgotten God's truth that "mercy triumphs over judgement"—and therefore, we don't know the power in affirming each other.

What's more, when you close off so fearfully to your need for mercy, it's hard to receive it once it finally comes. Davie taught me that it's one thing to tell someone what you like about them, but quite another thing for that person to accept it.

Staying open enough to be blessed, that is, means staying open enough to be hurt. It's an act of faith.

Years ago, I had a large potted plant in my apartment living room, which I watered semi-occasionally. One day, I returned from a trip and noticed it was drooping weakly—and the soil was rock-hard. To atone for my laziness, I immediately poured a whole canteen of water on it—and was shocked to see the water overflow the side of the pot and soak my carpet.

Like that unwatered potting soil, our human spirits dry and wither from lack of life-giving love and affirmation. If we don't face that unmet need and bring its awful pain to Jesus with tears, we cope by hardening our emotional defenses and shutting down to others. **Later, when God wants to open us up to something good, our walls have become so fortified that we can't receive it.**

And so we can't receive Father God's love. In fact, we crucify the One He sends to restore us.

Even as dry soil has to be soaked slowly and persistently, so most of us today are trapped by our own defenses—which as children may have protected us from harm, but now only shield us from love.

You can't often change someone else by criticizing. But you can change someone by speaking affirmation, namely, yourself.

Confessing to God that you haven't trusted Him to deal mercifully with your wounds and asking Him to open you up again to others, is a good way to start.

Telling others honestly and openly what you like about them is a good way to let Him continue.

21

The Easter Fish
Resurrecting the Boy

What human nature does is quite plain…. People become enemies and they fight. They become jealous, angry, and ambitious…. But the Spirit produces love, joy, peace, patience, kindness, goodness, faithfulness, humility, and self-control. (Galat. 5:19,20, 22,23)

"HEY, GORDON!" DAVIE EXCLAIMED, leaping up from behind the TV. A blast of stereophonic six-guns rang out as he galloped towards me, arms open. "How'd you know I was home all alone this afternoon?"

Smiling, I stepped through the front door and bent low for a hug. "Well, this is a good surprise," I declared, lifting Davie high and carrying him across the room. "I didn't even know you'd be here at all. Last week I came by twice and you were gone."

Davie frowned as I set him down and squatted in front of him, my hand on his shoulder. "Aw, Mom and Suzy keep wanting me to go out Easter shopping with them for clothes and all," he scoffed. "Finally they let me stay home today." A trace of pain softened his frown. **"I wish they'd do something for boys!"**

I shifted uncomfortably as Davie's father crossed my mind. Someday maybe we would talk together about his dad, but the time never seemed right. His sister Suzy was only two years older, but somehow she seemed to manage better.

All at once, horses screamed through a zing-burst of ricochets. Quickly, I reached around for the TV switch, as a dusty cowpoke sighted down his rifle. With a flip of the switch, he disappeared in a flash of darkness.

FISHING, NOT SHOPPING

"Well, I didn't come to take you shopping for girls' clothes, that's for sure!" I laughed. "Guess where I'm going?"

Davie's frown gave way to puzzled innocence. "Where?"

"Fishing!" I proclaimed, rising up triumphantly. "Want to go with me, right now?"

"You mean it?" Like a sportscar at a stoplight, Davie's body trembled.

"You bet!" I declared. "We'll leave a note for your mom and Suzy." I clapped my hands loudly. "Let's go—on the double! Get your jacket and old sneakers. We can share my rod and we'll be reeling 'em in any minute now."

Amid a flurry of zippers and shoestrings, I scribbled a note.

"Ready!" Davie announced moments later, and together we dashed out the door and jumped into my car. As the blocks whizzed past outside, Davie examined my bag of hooks and burlap fish sack on the floor. "When we get there, I'll carry the hook bag and fish sack, OK?"

"Great!" I chimed in. "You get the sack this time, because when we come back, the fish sack will be so heavy you won't be able to carry it by yourself!" I reached over and punched the boy playfully on the shoulder, and together we laughed.

A small department store appeared ahead on the right, and I pointed. "Hey, why don't we surprise your mother and Suzy with some Easter candy or something?" I said. "We can stop at that store for just a second."

"Oh, Gordon, no!" he protested, eyes flaring as if I'd betrayed him. "I don't want to do anything for them. Let's just you and me

go fishing."

Startled by his intensity, I drew back. "Well..," I hesitated, then shrugged. "If that's the way you want it, OK." The store disappeared behind us and I turned the corner.

"Gordon, look!" Davie shouted suddenly. "There's the fishing pier!"

HITTING THE BEACH

"Right!" Pulling into the parking lot, I stopped the car with a jolt. Like soldiers hitting a beachhead, together we scrambled out the doors.

"Got my stuff!" the boy reported, grasping the fish sack in one hand and the hook bag in the other.

"Me, too," I confirmed, grabbing the pole out of the back seat.

With a slam of doors, we beelined for the pier.

"See how fast you can walk without running!" I called out, picking up the pace. Straining and puffing, side-by-side we stiff-stepped onto the wooden deck and out over the breakers below. After a few yards we looked at each other and burst out laughing. At once, Davie sprinted for the railing at the end of the pier, and I broke into a run after him.

Together we reached the railing laughing and out of breath.

"I'm glad we ran to the pier," Davie said. "This way, we can catch lots more fish, huh, Gordon!"

Out of breath, I leaned the tip of our rod against an old notch in the scarred wood, and sucked in deeply. "Yeah, but forty years old's not eight years old!"

Like sweet pipe smoke, our laughter floated off into the clear ocean sky, until quietly, we gazed out over the breakwater and beyond. Enthroned on the horizon, the sun beamed and puffed billow-white clouds as an old salt breeze patted us on the shoulders.

"Let's catch one right away!" Davie burst out suddenly. "Let me do it first!"

"You bet," I said, handing him the rod.

Excitedly, he set the reel and pitched our lure toward the sky. Together we watched as the shiny steel winked at us in the sun, then plopped into the water below.

HOOKS, SHIPS, AND WHALES

For awhile, we wondered at how you can really see fish jumping right out of the water sometimes. Lures, we agreed, were sure easier than putting dead anchovies on your hook. Leaning out over the surf below, we talked about fish scales and sea water and rods and reels and hooks and ships and whales.

And then, we waited.

In the uncertain quiet, I looked down at the shell-crusted pilings below and sighed uneasily. "I'm glad you were home when I stopped by," I said finally. "This is fun."

"Yeah," Davie scoffed, a slight sneer curling his lip. "Everyone else just wants to go out shopping for Easter clothes."

I wondered: should I ask if he wanted to talk about his dad? I'd been seeing him almost two years now, but never felt sure how to approach so deep a wound.

Below, a swell nudged our line—and passed.

"Go easy on those girls," I said finally, with a good-natured arm-punch. "You know, that's your mom and sister you're talking about!" Hesitating, I added, "Maybe we could stop on the way home at least, and get them an Easter present or something."

The line relaxed as a receding wave sucked outward, then tightened as another rolled in. "No way!" the boy declared, gripping the rod furiously. "I'm never gonna do anything for *them!*"

Startled, I drew up. "You sound…pretty angry," I offered.

Turning away, he thrust his head over the rail to examine our line.

Suddenly, a flock of seagulls gathered above us beyond his ability to cast, and swooped low over the water, shrieking loudly.

"Look!" I cried out, pointing to the gulls with one hand and taking the rod with the other. "That means there's fish way out there! Let me cast out for us this time." Quickly, I reeled in and cast out again where the gulls were diving and splashing. As soon as it hit the water, the lure disappeared…and almost at once, the line jerked tight.

"A hit!" I shouted.

Davie leapt onto the railing. "You got one, Gordon!"

Pulling back on the rod, I glimpsed my taut line darting across the water like a laser beam. "He's a big one, too!"

"Hold onto him!" the boy yelled, bouncing excitedly.

Tugging firmly, I dipped my rod slack, reeled in several turns quickly, tugged and reeled again. All at once, a glint of silver swirled and broke the surface.

"There he is!" Davie shouted, pointing.

Feverishly, I reeled in as the fish reached the pilings below and popped out of the water. "Here it comes!" I burst out, jerking up and over the railing.

Glistening majestic in silver and blue, the fish flew high up and over the railing, caught the dying rays of sunset, then fell flapping wildly onto the splintered brown deck.

"It's a bonito!" I called out. "Probably a foot-and-a-half long! What a beauty, huh?"

As I rushed over and bent down to take the lure-hook out of its mouth, the fish flashed a clean row of needle-sharp teeth and slapped the wood planks furiously.

Startled, I drew back.

ANGRY FISH

"Wow," I said quickly, embarrassed. "It's sure angry, alright, isn't it?" I watched as the fish suddenly flopped and lay still, its gill flaps quivering.

"Well, we got one at last, didn't we, Davie!" I declared, staring at our prize. Suddenly, a splotch of red appeared just above the hook and trickled down onto the shiny steel lure. Gull shrieks trailed off in the distance as a ripple of conquest beckoned, then slipped off and darted away.

All at once, I realized that the boy hadn't said a word. I turned, and saw that he was staring, too.

"Davie?" I said.

Standing motionless, he looked at the fish.

"Davie...." I repeated, then paused uncertain. A gust of sea breeze nudged as I looked again at the trembling fish and then back at the boy. Awkwardly, I reached out and put my hand on his shoulder. "Are you...sad?"

"No!" he said quickly.

Turning, I followed his gaze. As we watched, the fish spread its gill flaps wide, lifted slightly, and then fell back quiet and still.

"I'm sad," I said finally, because I really was. "Are you sad, too?"

"Yeah," Davie murmured.

Together we stood there, watching sadly where our beautiful fish lay still.

"Bonito put up a good fight, don't they?" a husky voice broke in from the railing across from us.

"Oh...uh...yeah," I mumbled, gathering myself and bending over quickly to pull the hook out. Without looking at the boy, I tossed the fish in our sack, turned and cast out again hurriedly. Planting my elbows on the railing top, I leaned forward very casually until only the sun and the sea could see my face.

Beyond, the neat row of jagged breakwater stones gnashed at the incoming tide that burst foaming and white upon it.

I tried to piece things together. All I'd wanted was to show the boy some fatherly attention and maybe catch a fish or two. I usually don't catch many fish, anyhow. And even if I wanted to throw this one back, it was too late. Besides, I really did want it.

Glancing nervously over my shoulder, I saw the boy standing uncertain before the burlap sack as the old man across from us smiled approvingly.

A steaming platter of juicy bonito steaks flashed in my mind, and my stomach growled. Then, strangely, a piece of fried chicken popped into my imagination—and I saw myself seizing a chicken and wringing its neck as it squawked desperately. I grimaced and saw again the fish flapping on the deck: a perfectly ordered, un-manufactured, determined row of teeth from out of the ocean darkness.

Suddenly, I remembered a story about Native Americans who

always prayed when they killed an animal for food, asking the animal to forgive them and promising to use it only for their genuine needs. *Pagan stuff*! I scoffed, and turned back to look at the breakwater.

And then it struck me: *I hadn't prayed at all!*

Below me, a wave swept cleanly to the shore and broke with a dull roar. I sighed, reeled in my line, and turned around.

Pacing nervously along the railing, Davie was pretending to look out at the water. As I locked the reel, he glanced over at the fish sack.

PRAY FOR THE FISH

"Davie," I offered, "do you think...maybe we should say a prayer to God about our fish when we get home?"

The boy's eyes riveted on the sack. "Yes!" he snapped.

"That's a good idea," I declared, surprised at how quickly he agreed. I patted him on the shoulder.

Clearly, Davie was not into fishing anymore. *Still*, I thought, *as long as we're here, no sense in wasting the opportunity. Maybe there's some more fish out there like that one.*

Turning back to the ocean, I cast out again and waited. Before long, I knew it was no use.

"Ready to go?" I asked, reeling in at last.

Leaning quietly against the railing, Davie nodded.

I handed him the pole and took the sack myself. Without speaking, we re-traced our steps quietly to the parking lot.

The heavy weight of the fish surprised me as we walked. It was a big one, alright—two or three pounds, at least. Likely the biggest fish I'd ever caught. "We're lucky we had such a clear day for fishing!" I declared, grasping for connection.

Tight-lipped, the boy adjusted the pole in his hand and walked on.

I felt myself getting nervous, then angry. *Why was I so rattled over a simple fish? And how did I ever get myself into praying for it?* So far as I knew, neither Davie nor his mom and sister had ever even gone to church.

As the car appeared, I decided that the boy would probably let it slide anyhow.

"Wanna see if maybe there's a good movie on later tonight?" I offered brightly.

Davie knit his brow. "We're gonna have our prayer, aren't we, Gordon?"

I stopped. "Oh, well...sure, Davie, sure. Of course we're going to have our prayer." Stalling, I walked slowly to the car door, opened it, and then carefully arranged our gear and the burlap fish sack on the back seat. *Unbelievable!* I thought. *How did all this happen? Why couldn't he just ask me how a fishing reel works or something simple like that?*

And then, at last, we were sitting beside each other in the front seats. "Well...," I began, reaching into the back seat for the sack and laying it between us. Nervously, I turned and looked at Davie. "What shall we...say to God?" The boy's eyes darted anxiously to the sack.

SAD FOR THE FISH

Father, tell me what to say! I prayed quickly. "Why don't we... uh," I started, unsure—and then decided on the safe route. "...just tell God how we're feeling right now, OK, Davie?"

"We're sad," he blurted out, "...for the fish."

"Yes, God," I agreed. "We're really sad for the fish."

At that, a strange thought leapt into mind. Pausing, I added, "And God, I guess you're sad for the fish, too."

We sat quietly, looking at the burlap between us, crumpled and still.

I shifted uneasily and stumbled ahead. "What do you think would make God happy right now?" Instantly, I drew back at my words. *What a stupid question! Was I just trying to deny and escape my discomfort? I had absolutely no idea what would "make God happy" right then! Now I'd led the boy down a blind alley and...*

"I know," the boy was saying. "God would be happy if we shared the fish with Mom and Suzy."

My jaw dropped in amazement. Fumbling for words, I gestured

clumsily as if to speak.

My mouth closed. Nodding meekly, I reached out and grasped Davie firmly on his shoulder, with the manly gesture I'd saved for when he caught a fish. "Want to have Easter dinner together this Sunday—all of us?" I asked. "We'll have plenty of fish to go around!"

Davie looked up at me at last and smiled. "Let's go ask Mom!" he exclaimed, beaming. "I bet they're home now!"

22

The Dad Who Cried Wolf

Praying Dangerously for Your Child

Ask and you shall receive; seek, and you will find;
knock, and the door will be opened to you. (Matt. 7:7)

AT TEN YEARS OLD, MY SON WAS A GREAT WOLF FAN, and when in the summer of 2002 we jumped at last off the Alaskan Express at Denali National Park train station, his excitement became fierce. "They have real wolves out there in the park!" he declared, squinting with determination at Mt. Denali's snow-covered peak far off on the horizon. "I bet we'll see one!"

"That would be great, alright!" I noted, careful to measure my words and affirm, but not fuel his enthusiasm. The wolves were out there, alright, but the all-day bus tour we had booked for the next morning made no guarantees. I was just happy for these few days together with my son before speaking at a conference in Anchorage.

Later that night in our motel room, the boy poured excitedly over several local tourist pamphlets, each bearing majestic wolf photos in glorious color. **All, however, cautioned "not to expect to see wolves in the wild," but encouraged rather, to "find satisfaction" simply knowing that "such wonderful creatures are out there hiding."**

Not good news to a boy thousands of miles from his bedroom wallpapered with wolf posters, hoping to see the real thing. "The scenery will be great!" I declared gamely, each time we read a pamphlet disclaimer.

Noting that the tour bus left at 5 am, I rushed the boy into bed, hoping to short-circuit any further animated conversations on how great it was going to be to see "a real live wolf." The greater the anticipation, I figured, the greater the disappointment. I knew how much this meant to my son, and didn't want to see his heart broken— nor his faith.

SEND US A WOLF!

As we said our prayers together, I began by thanking God for our health, for bringing us to such a beautiful place, and "all the good things we're going to see tomorrow." Fully intending to end my prayer there, I suppressed a yawn—and was startled by the words that leapt unleashed from my mouth: "And Father God, send us a wolf tomorrow!"

With a start, I jerked up. The boy's eyes were closed, but it was too late. Like fireworks, the words had shot through the air and exploded in his heart.

"Yes, God!" he declared, his eyes bursting open excitedly. "Send us a wolf tomorrow! Amen!"

Quickly, I pasted a smile on my face. "Well, …OK," I managed, gathering myself and tossing him a pillow. "Now let's hit the sack." As we hugged goodnight, I felt his body tense with anticipation.

Oh no, Father, I prayed quietly, desperately. *What have I done? I'm sorry for going out on a limb like that. I know what the pamphlets said, but I guess I just want this so much for him that I got ahead of myself. Please cover my son and protect his heart!*

Neither of us slept well that night—for different reasons.

The next morning at dawn, we arose quickly, gobbled a banana amid handfuls of trail mix, and dashed out to the curb. There, an aging, semi-resuscitated school bus sat waiting pale and tan-painted, with about 50 others on board. Soon, we pulled away and turned onto a dirt road toward the mountains.

The driver, husky and dressed in safari khakis, spoke into his headset sound system with a deliberate, confident tone. Noting brightly that he hadn't seen "a day this clear in months," he hoped we would see "plenty of sights" as we drove out into the wilderness.

"I wonder when we'll see a wolf?" my son exclaimed, leaning eagerly into the window and scanning the terrain.

I said nothing.

The beautiful weather did indeed allow us to go a full 15 miles closer to Mt. Denali than planned, and when hours later we arrived at the turnaround spot, we had seen through binoculars snow-covered peaks, a distant mountain goat, several hawks, a fox, a gnat-sized grizzly bear miles away down a ravine, and last but frankly not least, several pit-stop bathrooms up close.

As eventually we turned and headed home, I stared uncomfortably ahead, trying not to look at the boy seated beside me.

"I guess that's all we're gonna see," he sighed at last, staring flatly out the window. A pause, and then he turned to me. "Do you think maybe we can still see a wolf, Daddy?"

Father, help! I cried out in my heart. "Well," I stumbled, struggling for an even tone, "of course…we don't know, but remember…I mean, the pamphlets said they…you know, don't come out too much."

SURRENDERED DISAPPOINTMENT

The boy's head drooped noticeably, and I pushed ahead. "Are you… disappointed?"

"Yeah," he acknowledged, turning back to the window—this time not to see, but not to be seen.

I patted him gently on the shoulder. "I know—we really wanted to see a wolf, didn't we?" Together, we sat there in surrendered disappointment, bobbing and leaning as our old bus bucked matter-of-factly along the bumpy dirt road.

Soon, the boy lay back limp against his seat and fell asleep.

I sighed in dismay. *Come on, Father!* I begged under my breath, with more than a hint of anger. *Bring a wolf to my son! We'll probably never get back here again in our lives, and if we do, he'll be too old to get excited like this. You made every last animal on this planet. You're*

Lord of all creation. You can do it!

Amid the growing shadows and coming sunset, my anger trailed off into sadness. *...please, Father?*

Scanning the hills on either side of us, I saw nothing. Slouching forward, I shook my head helplessly. *This is not going to be easy to explain, Father! But I give up. To you. I can't make it happen. It's in your hands. You're going to have to deal with this boy's heart when we get back!*

Again I sighed, and then, with a last, reluctant glance at my sleeping son, leaned back into my seat and determined to rehearse my presentation for the men's conference that weekend. Stressed and exhausted, however, I soon yielded to the drowsy hum of the bus engine, and drifted off.

"LOOK!"

The shout fired out, jolting me awake.

"Look! A wolf—over there, to the right!"

BOLD RELIEF

The bus lurched to a stop, and all necks stretched to see. Sure enough, only about a hundred feet off to the right—on our side of the bus—a large grey wolf stood out in bold relief before a white patch of snow. As the driver shut off the ignition and held his hand up to urge silence, I grabbed my son's shoulder and shook him.

"Wake up!" I whispered loudly into his ear, pointing outside. "It's a wolf! Right out there!"

Startled, the boy looked around, rubbed his eyes, and turned to the window. "Wow!" he exclaimed, and sat bolt upright. "It really is a wolf!"

The entire bus hushed with excitement. After a moment, the driver spoke up, his forceful tone now lost in humble wonder "And would you look at that!" he whispered amazed into his microphone, "coming over from the left!"

There, a second, dark-coated wolf was approaching the grey, bouncing along playfully—clearly younger. When the two met, the elder gave a subtle but clear lurch, whereupon the younger wolf pulled up and bowed down in submission.

We watched astonished as the "adolescent" then jumped about awkwardly and fell groveling on the ground, almost as if to demonstrate that he was a mere bumpkin and clearly no threat to the more distinguished, sober Alpha. Finally, he sat up and howled, maybe to impress—or praise?—his elder, and then bounded off in the distance.

Duly acknowledged, the grey turned in our direction and continued ambling along, right toward the bus. Excitedly snapping pictures, my son watched as the Alpha trotted in majesty before the bus and walked out ahead of us on the road. As his audience sat spellbound, the wolf sauntered off to the left and disappeared matter-of-factly behind an outcropping.

REVERENT HUSH

For some time after, the entire bus sat stunned in a reverent hush. If not for the bus seats, I would have fallen on my knees. I tried to pray, but found no words.

"Well, folks," the driver declared at last, his professional aplomb fading into awe, "what you just saw was…something very…very special. You just don't often get to see a wolf at all, much less two. It's been a couple years since I've seen one even at a distance, and never saw one come that close to the bus.

"I'm telling you," he declared, shaking his head in disbelief, "it'll be a long, long time before anything like that happens again." Slowly, with humble regard, he sat up in his seat and reached for the ignition key. "You need to know you're some very lucky people!"

As the bus coughed alive and chugged ahead for the final few miles home, I turned with a smile to my son, now beaming with joy. "Well, God sent us our wolf after all!"

"He sure did!" the boy exclaimed, "A real wolf—even two! Wait 'til I tell my friends back home about this!"

As he turned to examine his photos, it was now my turn to look away.

Father, what can I say? Your heart for this boy is…amazing. I was so worried for him. I guess… I just didn't believe you would do it. Forgive me for trying to cover up for you, as if that would preserve his faith. What can I ever do to thank you for what you did today?

Almost as soon as I asked, in my heart I sensed the words, "Tell the driver."

Tell the driver? Uncertain, I drew up. The driver had given no indication that he was a Christian, and his rugged, matter-of-fact manner suggested little exposure to church. Nevertheless, it occurred to me that in fact, his apparent inexperience with religion might offer an open door. Determined to honor my offer, **I resolved to overcome the fear and asked Holy Spirit to make me ready.**

Soon the bus arrived back at our motel. As everyone stretched and filed off, the driver stood at the door and shook hands with measured enthusiasm. Clearly, he wanted everyone to grasp how marvelous the day's experience had been, but knew that, as first-timers, they could only assume you see two wolves every day on this tour.

AWE-STRUCK

I waited until everyone else had left. Taking a deep breath, I walked over to him at last, and extended a handshake. "I want to thank you for the great job you did today."

Smiling—and still awe-struck—he nodded.

"That was great that we had the clear weather and got to see the mountain closer," I said, "but my son and I will never forget the wolves."

"Neither will I!" the driver declared. "I've been leading this tour for years and this is as good as it gets. You do this day after day and kind of get used to it—but I'm telling you, today was like nothing I've ever seen!"

"It was really special," I agreed, pausing to take another measured breath.

I pressed on.

"I…uh, I wanted to tell you that….my son and I are…well, we're Christians, and last night in our motel room—right over there," I motioned, pointing to the motel, "we were reading all the pamphlets about the tour and how we shouldn't expect to see any wolves. **But we prayed anyhow and asked God to send us a wolf today.** And we believe God brought those wolves to us."

Uncertain yet humbled by the day's experience, the driver lifted his eyebrows respectfully. Was that a flicker of recognition I saw in his eyes, a sense possible only in an outdoorsman so close to nature that indeed, all creation is subject to the larger Creator?

Resolutely, I reached and shook his hand once more. "Thanks again for your part in it all—you did a great job." With a nod toward my son, I turned to leave. "We'll remember this day for a long time."

Since then, I've wondered, Did my talk with the bus driver make any difference in his life? Did he ever become a Christian? Or was he just startled by this "religious nut"? I'll never know.

I do know, however, that as I waved goodbye to him and put a hand on my son's shoulder, I sensed another hand on my shoulder— and a reassuring voice in my heart: "Good job, son."

P.S. from God

Seven years after writing the above story, I'm back in Alaska for another conference, reconnecting over lunch with an old pastor friend I haven't seen in almost 25 years. As we chat, he asks me if I've ever been to Alaska before, and soon, I tell him my wolf story.

"Well, now, that's...really amazing," he declares. Hesitating strangely, he then shakes his head. He leans forward, about to speak further—but falls silent.

Assuming he's simply impressed by my story, I nod. "Yeah, it really is amazing, alright!"

I wait as he sits quietly.

"You know," he offers finally, uncertain but elated, "I don't think that's the end of your story!"

"What do you mean?" I ask, puzzled.

"Well, in the summer of 2004, two years after you saw your wolves, a pastor friend of mine visited from the Lower 48 and was all excited to see a grizzly bear in the wild. He had read about Mt. Denali, and figured that was the place to go.

"So I drove us there to the Park and we went together on that same rickety old school bus tour you went on. He really wanted to see a bear. Like your story, the mountain view was spectacular—but we didn't see any bears."

My friend smiles thinly, turns his head away for a moment, then looks back at me with a twinkle in his eye. "When we got off the bus, my friend was of course disappointed. The bus driver—a, self-confident, outgoing, rugged safari sort of guy—was going around saying goodbye to the riders and all, and eventually he came over to us and asked us how we liked the ride.

"The guy was a bit on the macho side—not really intimidating, but enough to make my friend unsure how to reply. He certainly never gave any indication that he was a Christian, and in fact, if you'd asked us, we probably would've said he wasn't.

"Anyhow, my friend decided to go ahead and be honest. He said that he was a pastor visiting from the Lower 48, hoping to see a grizzly bear. He said the scenery was great alright, but he was really disappointed we didn't get to see a bear."

Again, my friend shakes his head in wonder, then breaks out into a broad smile. "The bus driver wasn't defensive at all. In fact, he looked my friend square in the eye and said, 'Did you pray for a bear?'"

23

Mt. Rushmore Smiles
The Power of a Praying Dad

For we brought the Good News to you, not with words only, but with power and the Holy Spirit. (1 Thess.1:5)

SHORTLY AFTER HIS 12TH BIRTHDAY, my son sits in a living room crowded with some fifteen of his cousins as the large extended family Christmas gathering turns to play "Cranium," a parlor guessing-game. Since his mother, Mary, is the youngest among six siblings, he is the youngest present, some ten years younger than his next oldest cousin there. Graciously, the young adults have invited him to play with them.

We've come these thousand miles partly because I'm anxious for him, an only child, to connect with his relatives.

But now that hope seems slim. These are an educated, professional group with a healthy sense of competition likely to blow him out of the game. Squeezed low on the couch between two others, the boy is hardly visible. As the first up reaches for a Subject card from the game deck on the coffee table, the two lean forward intently, blocking out the boy behind.

SAVE FROM SHAME

Watching anxiously from a corner, I hold my breath as my heartbeat rises. I want to save my son from shame, which would only make him withdraw from this family. But for Dad to intervene would only highlight his immaturity and shame him worse.

The first up, a businesswoman in her mid-30's, draws a card, slides it toward herself face down on the table and then holds it closely, glancing down and noting to herself the item which she will challenge the others to guess. As she knits her brow and decides what clues to offer, desperately I ease around closer to the back of the couch and stand above my son to pray.

Father, draw him into the family! I beg under my breath. *Pour out your Spirit on him to overflowing, give him what he needs to get in the game with everyone else!*

"Let's see," the woman is saying, looking up from her card and glancing around the room furtively at the others. "It's…. smaller than the ocean, but bigger than a car."

The crowd falls silent and tense. Faces lean closer yet. Eyes narrow.

"Mt. Rushmore!"

Suddenly, surprisingly, the silence is broken.

All pause and turn to find the voice. Two on the couch shift to each side, revealing the boy behind them as the source. Everyone laughs quickly at this apparent comic relief. Gathering themselves, they turn back to concentrate on their guesses.

But the cousin holding the Subject card does not laugh. In fact, she sits transfixed, her jaw frozen open.

"How…how did you know?" she stammers at last, dumbfounded as slowly, she lays down her card face up. The words "Mt. Rushmore" sit matter-of-factly before the family.

"I don't know," the boy proclaims from deep in the couch, his voice sparkling with wonder. "It just came into my mind."

Amazed, the group stirs.

"Oh, wow—that's like, supernatural!"

"Hey, we've got a genius among us!"

"Do do, do do," another chants the "Twilight Zone" theme song from the old TV mystery show.

Heads shake, puzzled smiles pass from one to another as a confused hush falls over the group.

Finally, an uncle in his 70s, clears his throat. "Well!" he offers, eyebrows raised. "That was sure something, alright!" Gingerly, he reaches for the Subject card deck and begins shuffling it. "OK—who goes next to pick a card?"

I stand stunned behind the couch, watching.

SON ARISES

My son leans forward smiling, embraced by a burst of chatter and laughter as the two beside him shift apart to make room for him.

Catching myself, I back away amazed, and return to the corner.

Father, what in the world is ... but before I can finish my question, I know. *Oh Father, come on! Sure, I wanted to make my son feel part of the family. And yes, I asked you to give him quick respect among his older relatives. But did you have to be so graphic about it? I mean, I was expecting maybe something a little more subtle. A few close guesses would've been fine.*

But the Father is not subtle, nor withholding, when He wants to draw forth His child.

Get over it, Dad.

And keep praying.

24

Standby Alert for Dad
When You Can't Be There

The protector of Israel never dozes or sleeps.
The Lord will guard you; he is by your side to protect
you. (Psalm 121:4,5)

LEANING AGAINST THE FRONT WINDOW, I glimpsed his rear bicycle wheel disappearing around the corner, sighed deeply, and stood watching the emptiness.

The first day of junior high had come so suddenly. Walking him to kindergarten and first grade, then driving him to another school through 6th grade had sometimes been inconvenient, but I'd come to treasure those times together.

And now, the bicycle. Two miles, we knew, was not that far, and would be good exercise for him—plus a chance to secure his growing independence. The boulevard with two lanes in each direction made me hesitate, but it had both sidewalks and a white-striped bike lane on either side between traffic and parked cars. We had made a "recon expedition" together a week before school started, biking to and from the school, and it went fine.

Still, as I sighed again and turned to my office, I wondered.

MANAGING ON HIS OWN

Father, I prayed as I sat down at my desk, *you've got to protect him. I know he's too old now for a dad to walk with him, and he needs this experience of managing on his own. But it's a huge school, with plenty more to worry about even besides the traffic getting there. I have a job to do myself and can't be with him—or even praying for him— 24/7.*

Stymied, I paused, and in that moment my eye was caught by the tiny red light on my desktop CD player. The player was off, but this "Stand By" feature enabled the unit to save electricity from a full switched-On position and yet turn on instantly when necessary, without taking time to warm up.

Yes! I exclaimed. *That's what I want, Father—a "standby" function in my spirit. Keep my heart open on minimum energy attention when he's out of my sight. That way, I can go ahead and do my work, and when he does need my prayer and covering, you can switch me On immediately and get me praying right away!*

Brightly, I sat up, nodding in satisfaction as I turned on my computer. *OK, Father—he's in your hands, and so am I. I'll trust you to stir me whenever you need me to pray for him.*

It was a good day's work for me, and a good junior high start for my son. At times, those first days of adjusting to the new school seemed overwhelming for him, but toward the end of the second week, he was beginning to make new friends and come home excited about his classes.

One mid-afternoon into his third week, when I was wrestling at my computer with a particularly difficult book chapter, a thought of my son crossed my mind. I was inclined to let it slip by, but when a moment later I paused to think more about how I wanted my chapter to focus, he came back to mind. I turned aside from my computer screen to offer up a quick prayer, and surprisingly, was **immediately swept into a surge of determination that catapulted me into deliberate, heartfelt intercession.**

I called out to the Father to cover my son with His hand, claimed the Blood of Jesus over him, asked for warrior angels to sing praises over him, set the cross over him, and prayed fiercely in the Spirit for several minutes. Eventually, the passion subsided.

PUZZLED AND WAITING

Puzzled, I waited quietly. *What was all that about, Father?* I prayed. Waiting further, but sensing nothing more, I shrugged and turned back to my computer.

A few minutes later, the front door burst open and I heard one of my son's friends' voice: "It's OK, you're home now."

As I turned to get up out of my chair, the cry "Daddy!" rang out fearfully. Leaping, I rushed out to the living room. There, my son stood holding his bicycle helmet, his jeans ripped down one side, T shirt torn and arm bleeding slowly from a host of scratches.

"What happened?" I exclaimed, rushing to hold him.

"I... was riding in the... bike path," he stuttered in short breaths, shaking. "This kid... came up behind me... real fast... I swerved... out of his way... but... a car was parked there and... my handlebars hit the car mirror... and I fell down....in the street."

Oh, Father! I thought. *Cars speeding by at 40 miles an hour and he falls off his bike right there in the road!* Struggling to maintain my composure, I hugged the boy and whispered a "Thank you, Lord!"

After a moment, I thanked the other boy for being such a good friend, and when he left, I led my son into the bathroom to take care of his cuts—which thankfully, were not severe.

As we entered the bathroom, my heart was pounding in fear. *What if...* but no, I determined not to allow my mind to go there. Rummaging in a drawer for the antibiotic ointment and band-aids, suddenly it struck me: the "standby light"! At once, a flood of thanksgiving and praise overwhelmed me, and I fell on my knees.

JOLT FROM GOD

"I didn't tell you this," I said, looking up excitedly at my son, "but two weeks ago when you started riding your bike to school, I asked God to keep me on 'standby alert' and jolt me whenever you needed me to pray for you. Today, right when you were falling off your bike in the street, He did that.

"I just kind of thought about you about 10 minutes ago when I was working at my desk, and then before I knew it I was praying and praying for you. **I didn't know you were in trouble, but God did—and he got me praying when you needed His help!"**

It's amazing. What can you do in the presence of such love and power, but worship?

Just this: you can hold your child—and then let go thankfully to "the Father from whom all fatherhood in heaven and on earth derives its name" (Ephes. 3:14NIV footnote).

25

The Fireplace Lesson
Sex Ed 401 for Dad

*I am the Lord your God, who brought you out
of slavery. Worship no God but me....Do not commit adultery.... Do not desire...another man's wife....*
(Exodus 20:2,3,14,17)

HAIRY LEGS AND A PHONE VOICE MISTAKEN for Dad signaled
the time to talk again. Not about women, like last time, but about a
man's heart. I'd need to be up front about body parts and the mechanics
of it all. But before talking about the physical experience, I wanted my
son to see his sexuality from God's perspective.

I confess the occasion came not with my own bold initiative, but
with a letter from school. All 7th graders, it noted, would the following
week receive an hour's teaching in "Life Science." Noting that "sexual
material" would be covered, the paper allowed that parents who did
not want their child to attend could sign the enclosed form excusing
him/her to the library during that lesson.

NEW RELATIONSHIP

This mere slip of paper announced a new stage in my son's life—
and in our relationship. Holding it, I paused uneasily. Any sexual
material designed by the public school system would be obliged to

portray if not advocate a variety of behaviors that I could not as a Christian and caring father countenance for my son. **I didn't want him to get the wrong message on a topic with such life-impacting power as sexuality.**

But what were my options?

I could just do nothing, passively let him go to the program, and hope he's not harmed by it.

Or, I could sign the release form. The teacher would then call him out in front of the class to leave. Being publicly singled out like that among his peers, however, could harm him worse than whatever shame the program itself might induce.

I balked. Either option felt like abdicating my responsibility, even chickening out. Not wanting my son to be taught about sex from a secular view might be necessary, but not sufficient.

If my goal for him were to insure he make choices to further God's purposes for him, I would need to get involved, and give him the understanding and tools to do that. If I didn't, I had no grounds for criticizing the secular system, which obviously was designed precisely to fill that gap in doing what parents were unwilling to do.

As the old story, government Bureau of Engraving counterfeit detectors are trained by examining real bills. You can only tell a false bill insofar as you know what a true one looks like. In brazen naiveté—from billboards to music videos and explicit pornography— **our sexually addicted culture parades the counterfeits among us**.

I wanted my son as a young man to see through these commonly accepted lies. I wanted him to hear clearly from his father who loves him what true sexuality looks like, in order to discern the false.

I found my biblical license in the above introduction to the Ten Commandments. There, God proclaims that healthy sexual behavior flows out of caring, saving relationship with One who created us male and female. In the biblical faith, history is thereby the foundation of morality. **Those who remember that they owe their lives to God, like the early Israelites whom He delivered from Egypt, are the most likely to respect His decrees—not because they fear His punishment, but because they trust He knows what's best for them.**

Anyone who cares and loves you enough to save your life obviously has your welfare in mind. God's laws, therefore, are designed to protect and guide His children; not to deny pleasure, but rather, to save from pain. When you know your father loves you, that is, you do what he says because you know it's best for you.

SAFE BOUNDARIES

In Father God's biblical model, a father's license to speak boundaries into his child's behavior is based upon his commitment to the child's welfare. As in teaching my son years earlier to avoid trucks in the street, fatherly authority in that process lies not in your overwhelming power to threaten and punish, but rather, your God-given heart to protect and guide.

On becoming a seventh-grader dad, these sobering thoughts began to stir in my mind. Junior high was already here, and the days of innocence were passing quickly.

I remembered the Father's promise to me about his future in Chapter 13, and realized that the Father's words to me back then squared with His preface to the Ten Commandments noted above, and also His later New Testament word to the Hebrews—whom God was sending, almost like teenagers on the threshold of adulthood, out into a pagan world:

> As for us, we have this large cloud of witnesses around us. So then, let us rid ourselves of everything that gets in the way, and of the sin that holds onto us so tightly, and let us run with determination the race that lies before us. (Heb. 12:1)

To open our talk about sexuality and encourage his faith, I would therefore need to root him in the men of his heritage and how God had worked in their lives.

OTHER MEN'S SHOULDERS

"Your life is not your own," I wanted to communicate. "You stand on the shoulders of many men who came before you, and walk in the saving grace of the God who delivered them from death and destruction. You're responsible both to those men and to that God to receive what you've been given and make the very best of it in your own life as part of this holy generational chain.

"You're not alone in this, your journey of manhood. You're blessed to have God's word written in the Bible, by which you'll know His character and what He, your Creator, has determined best for you. And I, your father, will always be there for you when you need me."

I knew where I needed to begin. My son had quite literally been saved by God's hand from the womb, as described in Chapter 2. At least once, God had intervened supernaturally to avoid serious consequences in the lives of both my father and me.

Those stories were essential to his masculine roots in this world. I remembered Dad's blessing him the previous year when we'd visited, invoking our cloud of Dalbey witnesses from past generations and charging him as the very next man in that bloodline to uphold the integrity of our family. Also, some years previously, my cousin in Philadelphia had sent me photos of my great grandfather and grandfather.

With these resources, I felt prepared. The next day, before my son arrived home from school, I told Mary that I was going to talk to him about sexuality and then let him attend the school's sex education program. She supported me in that decision, and I asked her to pray for me, to do the Father's very best. Then I asked her to leave the house at that time so he and I could be alone together.

She agreed.

Later at home, after his snacks, I told him I wanted to talk to him about sexuality some more, and we sat down together.

First, I pulled out the photos and told him how hard these men of his heritage had worked to better their families and themselves. I played Grandpa's blessing CD and talked to him about some struggles of my own which God had walked with me to overcome. I explained to him why "Your life is not your own," then reassured him, **"You're not alone in your journey of manhood."**

I then told him about the spiritual nature of sexuality (see my discussion of "one flesh unions" in my book *No Small Snakes*), and warned him that the power it generates affects only his body, but his spirit as well. I emphasized that this is why he needed to pray and strengthen his relationship with Jesus as this power began to stir in him.

FIREPLACE LESSON

"Remember when you were a kid how much fun we had with the fireplace, roasting marshmallows and popcorn?" I asked. "Why did we light the fire in the fireplace and not the hallway, the garage, or the kitchen floor?"

"It'd burn the house down," he noted.

"Absolutely!" I exclaimed. "When you get close to a woman, your body will feel warm, like a fire starting inside you. God has designed marriage like a fireplace, as the right place for that fire to burn so it brings fun and warmth. **But if you burn that fire outside of marriage, it'll destroy your home.**"

When questioning convinced me that he had heard my "lessons," I asked him to get his Life Sciences textbook and turn to the gender anatomy section. I then explained how a man fertilizes the woman's egg. I said that this power of creation reflects the hand of the Creator and must therefore be submitted to Him.

Physical contact with a woman, I said, should therefore be gauged according to your commitment to her, and that's why sexual intercourse is reserved for a lifelong relationship. I told him that sexual contact opens your heart to the woman, and encouraged him to protect his heart until Father God drew him to a wife.

When all had been said and understood, I told him to go to the sex education program at school and see for himself what he thought of it. There would be no shame at all, I encouraged, if he wanted to talk that over with me. At last, I laid a hand on his shoulder and prayed for him to honor his desire for a woman as a blessing from Father God, and to talk to Jesus and/or me whenever he felt uncertain or confused about it.

I do not offer my experience here as "the only way to do it." The Father may guide you and your son in a different way. **The most important thing is your heart for your son's welfare and your trust in the Father of you both to lead you.**

WHAT ABOUT DAUGHTERS?

"But what about girls?" dads often ask me. "How am I supposed to talk to my daughter about sexuality?"

Here's Mary's advice: A father's job is not to talk to his daughter about women and female sexuality. That's for the mother or some other trustworthy older woman to do. **Rather, Dad needs to teach his daughter about men, how we think and regard women.**

The issue of how she dresses will likely come up. Keep in mind that women dress for other women as a way of gaining feminine esteem, and often are less concerned about how they look to men. A man, of course, doesn't get respect among other men by how he dresses, but rather, by his ability to demonstrate power—as in the athletic, financial, or professional arena.

Suppose, therefore, that your teenage daughter is getting ready for school wearing revealing clothes. Besides either seething quietly or raging at her, try this:

"Honey, I know you want to look good when you go to school, and I want to tell you now that I think you're beautiful. I'm sorry if I haven't told you that enough. You always have been beautiful to me, and you always will be. Not just outside, but in your heart as well. (Here, you can add specific character traits you admire and respect in her, with specific examples of how she has demonstrated those traits).

"Because I love you so much, **I want to talk to you for a minute not about yourself, but about boys, and how they think.**

"When you dress in that short skirt and low-cut blouse, all your girlfriends will probably say how hip and hot you look, so stylish and fashionable. But that's not what the boys are thinking.

"When a young man sees a woman dressed like that, he can't see much more than your body. That's the way men are wired. He thinks, 'She's looking for sex.' He doesn't see your heart. He doesn't care about any of your wonderful character traits I just mentioned, because the way you're dressed tells him all he needs to know about your character—and in his eyes, it's nothing worthy of respect.

"Honey, I want the best for you. Someday, I want you to have a husband who respects and loves you for the wonderful young woman you are, both inside and out. As your father, I would ask you, Please, go and look at yourself in the mirror and ask yourself, not What would my girlfriends think? but rather, what would boys think?'"

Again, this is no formula, but has to come genuinely, out of your heart for your daughter. When in doubt, check with your wife on how best to approach this delicate but essential issue.

Remember, the Father loves your daughter even more than you do. Be bold, step out, give Him something to bless. Whether she can receive it or not, your effort shows you care for her. She may thank you, or she may dismiss you. That's entirely up to her and out of your control.

But I can promise that Father God will honor your courage and faithfulness as a dad in behalf of His daughter.

26

Back to Beginnings
Kindergarten for Fathers

We're so proud of you; you're so steady and determined in your faith despite all the hard times that have come down on you. We tell everyone we meet in the churches all about you. (2 Thess. 1:4TMB)

WHO CAN BLAME A DAD for wanting to show off his son?

Only the dad himself, as it turned out. But I'm getting ahead of myself. I'll just say that kindergarten registration day was none too early to brag for me, who if you'll recall, am a writer and wordsmith.

A little history here.

While the word "Mommy" entered my son's vocabulary before "Daddy," nevertheless I was happy when very early he not only wanted to talk more, but also showed a natural, intuitive grasp of words. Shortly before his second birthday, in fact, he came to me one day confused and upset.

"Daddy...!" he blurted out, hesitating—his brow knit and eyes squinting in frustration.

"Yes...?" I offered.

The boy stood there strangely, mouth open in frustration, but saying nothing more.

For an uncomfortable moment I waited, giving him room to settle on his thought—and stifling a fear of whatever might be causing his upset. "Well," I said finally, "what…is it you want to say?"

"I want…to say it," he declared at last, struggling, "but…but I don't have a word for it!"

I sighed, relieved—and stoked. "Well, don't you worry one bit about that, son!" I exclaimed, smiling broadly. "You came to the right place. We're going to get you all the words you need!"

DAD'S JOY

To understand my joy here, imagine the son of a truck driver saying, "Daddy, I want to take a lot of things somewhere, but I don't have any way to carry them." Or the son of a doctor, "Daddy, I want to help sick people get better, but I don't know how to do it."

Bottom line is, my son got words. Many words. Joke books, riddles, a children's bible, chapter books, Scrabble and other dictionary games—and 24/7 lessons in how to break words down to their original meanings.

Some time later, one day after pre-school, he came to me puzzled again.

"Daddy," he asked, "is there such thing as 'luck'?"

"Hmmm…, that's a good question," I said, pausing uncertain. *OK, Father, you're on. What do you want me to tell him?* "Yes…, that's a great question, alright!" I allowed, stalling.

And then it hit me. "You mean 'luck' like when something good just happens by itself and nobody did anything to make it happen?"

"Yeah," he nodded.

We had read his bible together and I'd taught him that God is the source of all good things. "Well," I offered, smiling, **"we know that God makes good things happen. So there's no word in the bible for 'luck'!"**

The boy thought for a moment, then smiled himself.

His verbal skill eventually led him to enjoy reading as well, and after several years of his growing in language ability, I strode confidently into the kindergarten classroom on enrollment day. I was anxious to meet his teacher—and hey, not to overlook a chance for Dad to show off his son's talent where it would be appreciated most.

OPPORTUNITY LEAPS OUT

As luck would have it—or rather, by the apparent grace of God— the opportunity leapt out as soon as we walked in the door. There, a large poster board and crayon sign perched on a kid's chair directed, PLEASE SHUT THE DOOR.

Parents were filing in, and amid the temporary hush of uncertain newness, I knew I'd have to act quickly. Stepping away from the doorway and sign far enough for my voice to be heard over the chatter, I called out loudly to my son in the crowd, "See that sign over there, son?"

The boy looked. "Yes!" he called back.

"What's it say?" Ever so modestly, I smiled at the crowd of parents around us.

Examining the sign, the boy shouted out, "PLEASE SH-T THE DOOR!"—complete with the vowel "I" intruding where a "U" stood clearly and, along with everything else in that kindergarten classroom, manifestly shaken. Certainly, any son's lack of experience with four-letter words could be seen as a plus—but in that moment, it suggested a mixed blessing at best.

At once, heads turned, jaws dropped, conversations ceased abruptly, and brows furrowed in…well, amazement. Not, I'm obliged to note, at the kindergarten teacher's spelling, which was of course impeccable—but rather, at the accomplished vocabulary of this little boy standing proudly before the sign, smiling at his daddy.

An impending classmate of their very own children, in fact.

In that moment, luckily—or rather, most assuredly by the grace of God—the teacher saw that all were present. With a loud and hasty clearing of her throat, she announced that indeed, it was time to bring our group to order and proceed with the morning's agenda.

At least, her agenda.

Eyebrows raised in amazement lowered in relief as all turned from a red-faced dad to focus instead on the teacher.

All, that is, except one happy little boy, who skipped proudly up to his father.

Smiling sheepishly, I bent down and mussed his hair. "You're a good reader," I whispered. "...and we'll keep on learning new words."

My intention, you understand, was simply to lift up my son. Well, OK, after lifting up his dad first. All that really needs to be said here is, It didn't work, and I've asked God to forgive me.

FATHERLY ZEAL

One day not long after the embarrassing kindergarten incident, my son and I hit the break point when he asked about an upcoming holiday. With fatherly zeal, I noted that "holiday" is really a compound word from 'holy day', which originates in the Hebrew understanding that...

"Daddy, that's *enough!*" he burst out.

As I could see from his scowl, it was indeed enough. "OK," I conceded. "Sorry for overloading you. But if you ever need a word, you know where to come!"

Sure, I like to see my son do well. When he does, I tell him and others—as Paul publicly applauded the Thessalonian church—because I want him to be "steady and determined in (his) faith" when, like the Thessalonians, he faces his own "hard times that...come down on (him)" in this broken world.

But I've learned to release my son from the burden of my esteem and let him earn his own kudos appropriately in his own time.

Years ago on that day of kindergarten enrollment, the Father of us both had His own agenda—namely, to give me as a father an education which might best be described as elementary. On that day, in fact, my son and I entered kindergarten together.

The real teacher, of course, was the boy—as so often over the years before then and since.

May what he's taught me help you welcome and enjoy your own adventure of fathering.

Epilog
In My Son's Footsteps

I lead him to the trail and together we run

until he is gone

at the first turning.

(I have run this path since barely he walked,

my mighty hand and outstretched arm

to cover him.)

Awaiting now a second wind, a familiar branch ahead

is waving uncertain.

Ah! He has passed this way,

newly tossing aside its hindrances

and leaving the old growth to shake in wonder.

Above, the hill he has already left behind

Bids me shorten my step

and keep my

pace and

shuffle quickly

toward the

merci-

ful

plat-

eau

where the

trail waits open

at last like an outstretched arm and…

and….

emptied before me.

Again he is gone

and I bow my head.

Where, like a miracle,

in the very dust of my earlier runs

his footprints lead even ahead.

And I, who have set the pace

now leap to match his gait and sprint

Awkwardly

until it

is not mine

at

last and

I fail.

More graceful now in my own reach,

I lope through sweaty thoughts until

Yes!

Just ahead of me

the return trail

measuring the brush between us

brings him running back.

In good time, we will meet again at the trailhead,

after I have reached the last turning.

But for now, I am complete

as he catches my eye

And answers my outstretched arm with a nod.

"Father God, I sure like telling stories about my son!"

"So do I!"

Appendix A

Breaking Generational Patterns
Interview with a three-year-old father[11]

Q: What's the first step in becoming a godly father?

Gordon Dalbey: Actually, it's being a son—that is, knowing God as your Father and what it means to be His son.

Q: Why is this relationship with God as Father so important to dads today?

GD: I once asked 350 Christian fathers, "How many of you, when you first became a father yourself, did your own dad reach out to you—maybe a call, a letter, a visit—with any comfort, encouragement, support, or advice?" Only five hands went up.

To be a son, a man must have a father. The average man today, like his father, hasn't been emotionally and spiritually fathered for generations. **As a dad himself, he has few inner resources to draw on besides his own experience, and therefore can only treat his son the way his dad treated him.** A man is crippled as a father and can't grow beyond his past until he takes his father-wound to Jesus for healing (see my book *Sons of the Father: Healing the Father-Wound in Men Today*).

Q: How, then, does his father-wound affect a man when he becomes a dad himself?

GD: Without Dad's demonstrated love, a boy grows up thinking, "Dad doesn't value me. I must not be worth much." He doesn't feel like a real man—confident that he belongs in the world, with both a destiny and the power at hand to fulfill it. **He feels tremendous shame and anger at being abandoned and unequipped for manhood.** I believe that's why our prisons are bulging and our streets are unsafe. But it's also why most men are afraid to be dads and withdraw from their kids. We feel inadequate and unprepared as men, and we know our brokenness will show up graphically in our own children. We don't want to add to our shame.

Q: How can a man let Jesus heal his father-wound, and become a godly father?

GD: By praying, "Jesus, show me my father the way *You* see him." A boy sees Dad as the Great Protector and Guide. He's afraid to face his father's weakness and/or absence because it means he won't be safe.

A boy of the flesh, therefore, cries *from* his father's wounds, as when Dad hurts him. **A man of God, on the other hand, cries *for* his father's wounds, as an intercessor.** That compassion moves a man to identify with Dad and forgive him, to recognize and thank God for whatever he received through Dad. Connecting like that to his genuine roots in the world, a man is freed to get on with his true destiny—and thereby, to give his son a heritage in which to recognize and fulfill the son's own destiny.

Q: Can being a father help to heal a man's father-wound?

GD: Absolutely. Knowing the heart of Father God is what heals the father-wound. An honest man knows he doesn't have within himself the wisdom and strength his children need. When he goes to Father God for it in their behalf, he'll receive the Father's heart. As a man thereby sees his own heart grow for his children, he can understand Father God's heart for himself.

Q: What's it like being an older dad for the first time, with a pre-schooler at 50?

GD: I need to say first that I have a beautiful, godly wife who's a tremendously loving, wise, and persevering mother. That makes a huge difference.

It's just great being an "older" dad. I'm old enough at 50 to have made a lot of mistakes and, hopefully, have learned a few things. I'm still young enough to have energy to learn more, and my career has developed by now to where I can pretty much set my own schedule and get time to enjoy my son. I take that as a rare privilege, and a responsibility to use it to help the many younger dads who don't have it.

Appendix B

Effective Single Dads[12]
Overcoming Popular Myths

It's hard enough being an effective father when your wife is around to help, but being single makes it even harder. If you're willing to look honestly at your situation, however, you can avoid the popular misconceptions today about being a single dad.

Above all, remember that God's truth is always balanced with grace (see John 1:17). If you feel unprepared and inadequate as a dad, welcome. Being a father humbles all men. Superman wouldn't look so self-assured with baby spit-up all over his cape! Yet it's that humility which allows you to identify with your child—and draw upon Father God's limitless grace for us who bear his title of "Father" (see Matt. 18:4ff).

Let's take a look at some of these myths, and the truth that sets us free to be the dads we want to be and our children need.

MYTH # 1 : "Single dads don't matter."

At 41, Steve had been divorced a year and his children were living several hundred miles away with their mother. "My ex-wife and I argue all the time," he told me. "Every time I call, my teenaged daughter Hanna jumps on the bandwagon and lashes out at me." Wounded, and wondering if his input really mattered, Steve had decided not to call the girl anymore, "until things settle down."

I told Steve I could understand his not wanting to stay connected to his daughter when she just hurt him like that. Being a man, however, means taking risks, and following Jesus means being willing to risk pain unto death in order for God to accomplish His purposes in and through you.

I therefore encouraged Steve to stay in contact with his daughter, no matter how painful her rejection. I suggested he write a letter to Hanna once a week—such as every Wednesday—nothing too heavy, but being sure to say 'I love you' and showing an interest in her school, friends, and activities. I asked him to commit to not expecting anything in return from his daughter.

Understandably, Steve balked. "But what if I do that and she's still angry at me?"

"Don't be misled by a child's anger," I told him. "Every child longs to be close to Daddy." I also explained that Hanna's anger was a common cover-up for her hurt feelings at being an innocent victim of the divorce—which would likely fade as she found him trustworthy through this painful time. In fact, the Bible describes Father God's heart for us, His children, with the Hebrew word *hesed*, meaning "persevering love" (e.g., Psalm 118:1-4).

Finally, **Steve agreed to surrender his own pain for the sake of his daughter.** After months of weekly letters, eventually she began to open up to him. "When I called yesterday to talk to her mom about some things, Hanna answered the phone," he told me excitedly. "Instead of just blowing me off and handing it to her mom, she said, 'Hi, Dad'!"

That was all his daughter said. But to a wounded dad, it was a tremendous boost. Steve is now a pastor, and recently—years later— enjoyed the deep satisfaction of performing his daughter's wedding. That's the influence of a loving, persevering single dad.

Dare to remember as a boy how much you wanted and needed your own dad. Your children want and need you just as much. Get prayer and counseling to resolve any anger or hurt feelings toward their mother, and determine to stay connected to your child.

MYTH # 2: "Solo fathers are on their own."

Among men with children under 18 years old, over 9 million

fathers do not live with their children and over 2 million live with their children but without a wife, according to the National Center for Fathering. A recent census reported that 24 million children today in the US do not live with their biological father.[13] That's a lot of company for single dads—and a large pool of resources you can draw from.

Many men in your own church are likely single dads. Why not call some of them and get together to talk things over? Feeling like you're the odd man out breeds shame—which goes away when you realize you're all in the same boat (see Romans 3:22-24). You may want to include married fathers in your discussion to broaden your range of resources.

Sure, reaching out to other men like that takes courage—but that's part of being a man. **You'll feel more manly when you join other men for support and encouragement.** You may hear a voice inside you saying, "But real men don't do such things!" And that, of course, is precisely why we get into trouble on our own! What real men don't do is pretend they're OK, hide their wounds, and run away from their children. (see "The Wolf Loves the Lone Sheep" in *Sons of the Father*).

MYTH #3: "Single dads can't be real fathers—or real men."

The first step in being an effective dad is to be a real man.

My definition of a "real man" is simple: A real man is a man who's real. He doesn't want to waste energy hiding from the truth that would set him free. He wants to face himself honestly and get on with what God put him on earth to do. As King David cried out, "Search my heart, O God, and find out what wickedness there is within me and lead me in the everlasting way" (Ps. 139: 23,24).

Unlike David, the media's tough, cool macho character is no real man, but only a fantasy designed to cover up the shame we feel for not measuring up as men. Ultimately, that deception keeps us from facing our need to get real with God and with other men.

Years ago, when Mary told me she was pregnant, I was excited— but scared. At my next conference I asked 350 Christian dads, "When you first became a dad, how many of your fathers encouraged you with helpful advice—maybe a phone call, visit, or letter?"

Only five hands went up.

If you're uneasy about being a father, welcome. We're in this together, and together we can go through it—even enjoy it—if we decide to get real.

Talk with other dads and ask them what they've learned. Why waste time and energy re-inventing the wheel, when other men have struggled through the same issues and can share with you what they've learned?

MYTH # 4: "Being a father is just about doing your duty."

Self-doubt seems to come with being a dad. Can I make enough money to support a larger family? With everything else on my schedule, how can I spend enough time with my child? Can I meet my child's needs?

These are real issues. But first and foremost, Father God wants to overwhelm you with the joy in being a dad. Listen to how He introduced Jesus to the world: "This is my son, chosen and marked by my love, delight of my life" (Matt. 3:17TMB).

Father God delights in His child. Do you?

Granted, since a child looks up to you almost as God Himself, the role can seem intimidating. Like most men, I balked at first. At times, I still do. Amid the pressing duties of fatherhood I need refreshment from life's Source. God provides just that in our children themselves. The humble, open child restores innocence and makes you feel like a kid again, able to receive. That's why, for Jesus, the child is the very gateway to the Kingdom of God (see Matt. 18:1-3).

"The best way to learn how to enjoy life," as a wise man once said, "is to rent a 7-year-old boy and take him to the zoo!"

Out in the living room, when I shut down my computer after writing these words, a boy with a twinkle in his eye is waiting to pounce on me like a lion. We'll roll around on the floor, roaring and wrestling, tickling each other and laughing ourselves silly. No matter how much the world may dismiss me, to my child I'm the King of the Universe.

The joy of fatherhood is the fountainhead of its tasks. Men who have forgotten this were not enjoyed by their dads.

Not to be enjoyed by your father is a terrible loss, often as bad as any punishment he could mete out. When a man doesn't enjoy his child, he not only misses out on one of life's greatest pleasures, but he communicates to the child, "You're not enjoyable. You're nothing to get excited about, so there's no use in your trying to do anything special or exciting with your life."

Sure, take care of your responsibilities as a dad. But instead of dwelling only on duties, look for a balance and make time to have fun with your kids. Take them to the beach, to an amusement park, the zoo, a natural history museum, a walk in the woods. Wrestle and fly toy planes with your son; dance and play tea party with your daughter. Let the child restore your joy in life—and let that father's joy in you lead you into knowing how much your Father God enjoys you as His child.

MYTH # 5: "Quality time counts more than quantity time."

Of course, not living with your children makes it hard to spend extended time together. Our fast-paced, high-energy society often snuffs out life's simple pleasures and deepest connections. But just as a farmer can't rush fruit to harvest, real relationships take time to root and grow.

While the popular talk about "quality time" may make you feel better, it won't secure your kids' bond with you. Sure, Disneyland weekends together can be fun. But Mickey Mouse can't heal the hurt from not being with each other.

Don't worry if you can't come up with an exciting plan for your time together. Whenever possible, spend unstructured, slow-paced time just hanging out with your kids. Go for a walk or read a book together. Sit in front of the fireplace and tell stories about your childhood days. Let your kids help you wash the car, clean the yard, or do other everyday tasks together. Relaxed quantity times such as these will open your heart to your children, and their hearts to you.

Single dads, you can become effective fathers by not buying into society's self-defeating myths. **You matter to your kids, big time.**

To keep that truth in sight, spend time with your Father "from whom all fatherhood in heaven and on earth derives its true name" (Ephes. 3:15 NIV *footnote*). To keep Father God's grace in sight, know that no man gets it perfect. Sometimes, you'll pray and talk to trusted brothers but still won't know what to do.

Welcome to this fallen world. Do your best—and trust your Father for the rest. Give Him something to bless. Remember, you're His son. As you call out to Him, He'll be with you—and give you what you need as you talk to Him about it and step out in faith.

You'll be glad you did.

And so will your children.

"Remember," God promised as Joshua led His children Israel into the unknown, "that I have commanded you to be determined and confident! Do not be afraid or discouraged, for I, the Lord your God, am with you wherever you go" (Joshua 1:9).

Do Pirates Wear Pajamas?

Chapter Small-Group Interaction Questions

Foreword

1. What did the author's father mean when he said, You want your son to have the best instead of giving him the best? Give an example of the difference from your experience as a dad.

2. The boy says a true adventure always stirs some fear. Tell about an experience you've had with your child that qualifies in that sense as an adventure.

3. What experiences have been part of your "labor pains" as a father? What have you learned from them?

Introduction

1. The author says that a child is "upsetting…when you cling for security to your own controlled agendas." Tell about a time when a child upset your controlled agenda. How did you react? How do you wish you had reacted? If those two answers are different, how did you learn to think differently about it?

2. Tell two valuable things that you learned about being a father from an older man before becoming a father yourself.

3. Can you think of a blessing you've experienced as a dad that your own father missed out on? Why didn't he experience it?

4. Can you think of a blessing your own child has experienced that you missed out on when you were his age?

Chapter 1

1. Why does Jesus say a child is 'the greatest in the Kingdom'? In what ways does our culture a) affirm that, b) deny it?

2. What does "responsible" mean literally? How is that different from the way most of us adults think? Have you ever seen your child act more responsible than you? What would it take for you to become

more responsible yourself now?

Chapter 2

1. How much did you get in on the action as a dad during the pregnancy, when your child was in the womb? What advice would you give new dads about that?

2. In what sense did the author lose his child at birth? As a dad, how have you experienced "losing your child" in that sense? What's that been like for you—easy? hard? Give an example from your experience.

Chapter 3

1. How much did you get in on the action as a dad when your child was an infant? From your experience, what advice would you give new dads about that time?

2. At what point did you begin to feel like a father? Did anything happen to kick-start that?

3. What did your wife think about how much you participated in parenting during those early times? What advice about that would you give young couples having their first child?

Chapter 4

1. Why did the author love his son? What did that teach him about God's love? Why do you think something so simple as that is so hard to learn?

2. Why did Father God bless Jesus as His son before Jesus did anything to earn that? How is that different from the way the world thinks? What do you think about it? Did you ever receive that kind of love from your own dad? Have you ever felt it for your own child?

3. Give an example of a time when you "corrected" your child and

    a) wish you'd done it differently

    b) were glad you did it that way

What makes the difference?

Chapter 5

1. Did your own father ever discipline you in a way that made you afraid of him?

2. Like the author, have you ever disciplined your own child and then thought differently, and were able to make up for it?

3. How have you disciplined your own child differently from the way your dad disciplined you as a boy? Why?

Chapter 6

1. Have you ever felt ashamed of the way your child was acting in public? Or at least, been afraid of how he or she might act? How did you handle that?

2. Have you ever been aware that your child wanted to do something innocently but it would be dangerous—like the author and his son's wanting to touch a truck? What options did the author consider about how to handle that? What do you think about what he finally did?

3. What's the hardest thing for you about "disciplining" your child? Have you ever seen your child internalize your discipline by using it to help others, like the author's child after play group?

4. If you want to discipline your child for his/her own protection, how can you do that without making him/her feel ashamed?

5. Where do you need grace as a dad?

Chapter 7

1. Why do you think a boy wants to imitate his father?

2. Tell about a time when you saw your child imitate you

    a) in a good quality of yours

    b) in a not-so-good quality of yours

3. Can you remember a time as a boy when you imitated your father? Do you do that in any way even today as a man?

Chapter 8

1. Have you ever seen your son imitate with girls his age the way you treat his mother?

2. When did you first see your son treat girls differently from how he treats boys?

3. Did you ever talk to your son as a little boy about girls?

4. When did you become aware as a boy that you were different from girls? Did your father talk to you about that? Were you ever aware that you treated girls like your dad treated your mother?

Chapter 9

1. Tell about a time when you realized your son's mother didn't understand boys. Did you try to explain to her what a boy needs and advocate for him? If so, how? If not, why not?

2. If a whole generation of boys grew up without a father to testify in behalf of his masculinity, how do you think that would affect the culture?

Chapter 10

1. Tell about a time when you protected your child from physical danger.

2. Tell about a time when your own father (or some older man) protected you from danger as a boy.

3. When you tell your child not to do something, how much of that is because his doing it makes you uncomfortable or because you want to protect him/her from danger? Has your child ever resisted when you wanted to protect him/her?

4. How did the author protect his son's heart when the boy was sad about his friend leaving him? Have you ever protected your child's heart? Can you think of other ways to do that?

Chapter 11

1. Do you think there's a "father instinct"? If so, what are some of the ways it might manifest? Have you ever experienced it?

2. Do you think many men recognize it? If not, why not? What effects could it have if more men did recognize it?

Chapter 12

1. Have you ever tried to accomplish something in front of your child and blew it? If so, how did you deal with it?

2. Like the author, do you share any characteristics with your own father that might embarrass you?

3. I (GD) asked a group of women, "If someone tells you, 'You're just like your mother', do you take that as a positive or negative?" Almost all the women agreed it was a negative thing. When I ask men how it feels when someone tells you, 'You're just like your father', most say that feels positive. Why do you think it's different for men and our fathers? What about you—would you take it as positive or negative?

Chapter 13

1. Did your dad ever tell you exciting stories about things he did as a young man? Give an example. How did it feel to hear that story? Did you identify with your dad at all in his story? Did you ever want to do something yourself like he did?

2. "In order to grow into your destiny, you need to root in your heritage." What does that mean to you? Do you agree? If so, what can a man do to root more deeply in his heritage? What do you know about your men ancestors that's part of you today?

3. What could you do to root your son in his heritage?

Chapter 14

1. Why at first was the boy in wonder of the girl, and what later scared him about her?

2. When was the first time you saw your son notice girls? How did you respond?

3. Have you ever talked to your son about how girls affect a boy? If not, what do you wish you'd said? What do you think a boy needs from his dad most when he begins to notice girls? What did you wish your dad had done for you then?

Chapter 15

1. As a boy with your own dad, was it easy or hard to have fun with him?

2. Were you ever able to speak into your father's life and tell him about something he was doing wrong? If so, what happened? If not, why not?

3. Has your child ever taught you to have fun when you otherwise wouldn't have? Was that easy or hard for you? Why?

Chapter 16

1. Have you ever noticed something good your son likes to do, and encouraged him to do it?

2. Have you ever tried to make your child do something you thought was good for him/her, but he/she resisted?

3. How can you tell what God is doing in your child? What are some ways to bless that in him/her?

Chapter 17

1. How much have you told your son about his grandfather and other men in his blood line before you? How could you do more of that?

2. What character traits did you admire most in your father? How

could you talk to your son about that as his heritage via you?

3. How is your son different from your father? What would you like most to give to your son that your dad never got from his father?

Chapter 18

1. When the author told his son that he was scared, the son was encouraged and leapt ahead. Why?

2. Did your dad ever tell you about something that scared him? What was it? How did it make you feel to know about it?

2. Have you ever told your son something that scared you? Was that easy or hard? Why?

Chapter 19

1. When you turned 11 or 12, did your father talk to you about sex and reproduction? If so, what did he say? If not, what do you wish he'd said?

2. Have you ever talked to your son about it? What input might be helpful from his mother on the subject?

3. Why is it hard to talk to your child about sex? (see *Pure Sex: The Spirituality of Desire* by Gordon Dalbey with Mary Andrews-Dalbey, PhD at abbafather.com)

Chapter 20

1. James says "Mercy triumphs over judgment." (2:13) Do you believe that? If so, give an example of how it's been demonstrated in your life.

2. Did you ever feel judged as a child? If so, how did that affect you?

3. Have you ever judged your child? How can you avoid judging your child? How can you overcome the effects after you do it?

Chapter 21

1. How can some adult male besides a boy's biological father help

him grow into manhood?

2. How did other men besides your blood father help you growing up? Give an example.

3. Have you ever called on other men to help your son grow into manhood? How could you do that?

Chapter 22/23

1. When you were a boy, did your dad or any other man ever pray for something specific in your life? If so, what happened?

2. What does the term "praying dangerously" mean to the author? What's the risk?

3. Have you ever prayed dangerously for your child? What happened?

4. How could you do that now?

Chapter 24

1. What does "standby alert" mean to you as a father? Have you ever felt yourself prompted to pray for your child when you wouldn't otherwise have thought to do so? What happened?

2. Have you ever asked Father God to set your spirit on standby alert for your child? If not, what do you think about doing so?

Chapter 25

1. What was the author trying to teach his son in "the fireplace lesson"? Do you think that's helpful or not?

2. Why does the author begin teaching his son about sex with stories about the boy's masculine heritage?

3. Why is it important for a dad to teach his daughter about men? If you have a daughter, how could you do that? (see "Fathers and Daughters" in *Healing the Masculine Soul*)

Chapter 26

1. Have you ever bragged about your child publicly? How did that

work out?

2. What does it mean to release your son "from the burden of (your) expectations," as the author came to learn? How can a father do that? How does it affect a boy if his father doesn't do that?

3. What has your child taught you that you appreciate most?

Epilog

1. When have you seen that your son is different from you and has his own life? How can you affirm him as his own person and still have a close relationship with him?

ABOUT THE AUTHOR

paperbacks, audio cd/mp3 at www.abbafather.com

ebooks at www.kindle.com

GORDON DALBEY'S widely acclaimed classic *Healing the Masculine Soul* helped pioneer the men's movement in 1988 and is still a bestseller today, with French and Italian translations. A popular speaker at conferences and retreats around the US and world, he has ministered in England, Hong Kong, Australia, New Zealand, Italy, France, Switzerland, Canada, and South Africa. A former news reporter (Charlotte NC), Peace Corps Volunteer (Nigeria), high school teacher (Chicago, San Jose CA) and pastor (Los Angeles), he holds an M.Div. from Harvard Divinity School, an M.A. in journalism from Stanford, and a B.A. from Duke.

Gordon has appeared on many radio and TV programs, including Focus on the Family. He lives in Santa Barbara, CA, and may be reached at www.abbafather.com.

Other Gordon Dalbey books
paperbacks, audio cd/mp3 at www.abbafather.com
ebooks at www.kindle.com

> Both refreshing and upending, Gordon Dalbey's books for men take us to depths of authentic manhood where we're humbled by its mystery and engaged by its call. Apart from either violence or lust, these books restore both courage and passion to manhood. Here's a masculinity you can trust—and the Father who makes it happen.

Healing the Masculine Soul

Today, politically correct voices cry out for men to be more sensitive, to tame our masculine nature. Meanwhile, the media bombards us with "macho" images of violence and lust. Is it any wonder men today are left bewildered about what manhood really is?

This pioneering, bestselling classic gives men hope for restoration by showing how Jesus enables us to get real with ourselves, with Him, and with other men. Its refreshing journey into the masculine soul dares men to break free from deceptive stereotypes and discover the power and blessing of authentic manhood.

Sons of the Father
Healing the Father-Wound in Men Today

"When you became a dad for the first time, did your own dad reach out to you with support, encouragement, or helpful advice?" Out of 350 Christian fathers, only 5 hands went up. "When you were 11 or 12, did your father talk to you about sex and relating to women?" I asked another gathering of 150 Christian men. Two hands.

Men today suffer a deep father-wound, which has left us unequipped for manhood. The father of Lies capitalizes on its shame and blackmails us into isolation, denial, and a host of bogus cover-ups—from money and guns to alcohol, sex, and performance religion.

The true Father of all men has come in Jesus to draw us back to Himself and to the man He created you to be. Here's the map to get you there.

Fight like a Man:

A New Manhood for a New Warfare

9/11 revealed the enemy of God and humanity as rooted in shame-based religion. The focus of warfare has now shifted dramatically from military battles to the hearts of men.

This trail-blazing book focuses on the crippling byproduct of fatherlessness in men today, namely, shame—too often fostered by religion, always overcome by Jesus. It's not about how to be a man, but knowing the Father who rescues and restores men. It's not even about how to be a warrior, but surrendering to the Commander of the Lord's Army.

Here, you won't be exhorted to obey, but invited to trust. You won't be commanded to do it right, but freed to be real. You won't be warned to be strong, but promised your Father's strength as you experience the grace and dignity of being His son.

> The awful wounding of our times, from family breakups and sexual confusion to drugs and violence, has left us hungry for a faith that embraces reality as graphically as we're forced to in this increasingly lost and broken world.

No Small Snakes

A Journey into Spiritual Warfare

This is my upending personal story of meeting and learning to overcome the powers of evil as portrayed in the Bible.

The problem in confronting spiritual reality, I discovered, is not that our childish imagination gets hooked into foolish fears, but that something real is evil and we can't control it. This humbling truth stirs shame in our Western, control-oriented culture and we deny the reality of supernatural evil. But pretending there's no thief in your house doesn't protect you from being robbed; it only gives thieves free rein to steal whatever they want.

In Jesus, God has invited us to exchange the illusion of our control for the reality of His power. This book extends that invitation to you.

Gordon Dalbey's books will stir you to a faith both passionate about its truth and compassionate in its grace. Here's freedom from universal tolerance on the one hand and narrow condemnation on the other—and Jesus at work today as God's vital Third Option to the world's self-defeating enmity.

Broken by Religion, Healed by God

Restoring the Evangelical, Sacramental, Pentecostal, Social Justice Church

This is my story of how I became born again among Evangelicals, discovered the sacrament among Catholics, was baptized with Holy Spirit among Pentecostals, and transformed by social justice ministries among Oldline Reformers. But it's also about the crippling brokenness in the Body of Christ today, which that journey revealed— how the Church has divided itself by these four very ways people meet Jesus, sabotaging its credibility and mission.

The same spirits of shame and division which animated the Pharisees and 9/11 terrorists have for centuries distracted Christians from what Jesus is doing and kept us from seeing each other as He does. Here's how to join Jesus as He battles unto today to heal His broken Body—and through it, this broken world.

Religion vs Reality

Facing the Home Front in Spiritual Warfare

Go figure out what this scripture means: "I'm after mercy, not religion. I'm here to invite outsiders, not to coddle insiders." (Matt. 9:13,14TMB)

Since Jesus, religion is obsolete.

Religion is our human effort to cover the shame of our sin-nature. Honest human beings know it doesn't work. In fact, that's why Jesus came—not to cover our shame but to remove it. He thereby revealed religion as a tool of the enemy to distract us from His work.

The power of evil unmasks this false security of religion. And so our sophisticated Western pride denies the reality of evil because it reminds us we're not in control. Tragically, we thereby forfeit the power to overcome it. Here's how to reclaim that power.

Chapters focus on works of the enemy often hidden by popular culture and religious denial. Titles include Facing Spiritual Denial, 9/11 and the Spirit of Religion, Ball Games and the Battle for Men's Souls, Homosexuality and the Father Wound, White Racism and Spiritual Imperialism, Unmasking Halloween, Overcoming Depression, and Delivered from Abortion.

Pure Sex

The Spirituality of Desire

There's more to sex than mere skin on skin. Sex is as much spiritual mystery as physical fact. (1 Corinth. 6:16,17TMB)

Today's quest for "sexual freedom" has misled us into a vast wilderness of options where we've forgotten what sexual desire is, where it comes from, how it was designed to function, and where the power comes from to fulfill it. Christians, meanwhile, have banned sexuality from church, leaving a vacuum which the world is literally hell-bent to fill. "Sex is dirty and immoral," as the culture confounds, "so save it for marriage and the one you love most!"

Here's the trailhead to authentic sexual freedom: not the absence of restrictions, but the presence of Father God, who enables its authentic fulfillment. Chapters include Sex as Holy Nostalgia, The Genesis of Modesty, Homosexuality and History: A Perfect Storm, Spiritual Consequences of Sexual Union, Sexuality and Religion: A Marriage Made in Hell, Controlling Uncontrollable Desire, Was It Good for You (Too)? Sexual Bonding and a Woman's Heart (Mary Andrews-Dalbey PhD).

Loving to Fight, or Fighting to Love

Winning the Spiritual Battle for Your Marriage

with Mary Andrews-Dalbey, PhD

"God created man in his own image,…male and female he created them" (Gen. 1:27)

Our spiritual enemy's most deliberate efforts to distort the image of God focus on His most fundamental reflection in this world—namely, on the union of "male and female." Amid this widespread attack on marriages, the divorce rate among Christians is the same as among others at about 33%. Clearly, the overcoming power God has given to His church is not being widely received and exercised by Christian couples.

"They say marriages are made in heaven," actor Clint Eastwood once commented. "So are thunder and lightning." In this fallen world, storms come to every honest couple. Those who fight in the power of the flesh think the question is, Who's right? But for those who fight in the power of the Spirit, the question is, What's God trying to teach us? It's not about how to make your marriage work, but how to let God work in your marriage.

Chapters include Never Waste a Good Fight, Leaving Father and Mother: The Trailhead to Marriage, For Better or Worse: A Woman's View (Mary), When You're Hot You're Hot; When You're not, It's Time to Talk about Sex, Fire Prevention: How to Stop a Fight before it Starts, and A Couple's Guide to Spiritual Warfare.

Endnotes

1   "Of course pirates wear pajamas," my cousin Jeff wryly observed. "Where do you think we got the term 'long johns'?"

2   Christeena Kale, instructor at HRock Church School of Supernatural Ministry, offered this insight.

3   Based on my article, "The Cry for Daddy," *Focus on the Family* magazine, 9/96.

4   S. Adams Sullivan, *The Father's Almanac* (Garden City, New York: 1980), p. xv.

5   Bill Johnson, *When Heaven Invades Earth: A Practical Guide to a Life of Miracles* (Shippensburg, PA: 2003), p.41.

6   Based on my article of this title in the *Santa Barbara News Press*,

7   Based on my article, "Defining, reclaiming the 'father instinct'," *Santa Barbara News Press*, 6/21/98.

8   First published in *New Man* magazine, 9/96.

9   *Santa Barbara News Press*, 6/20/99

10   *Santa Barbara News Press*, 6/18/00

11   *Today's Father* magazine, Vol. 3, #2-3, 1995, p. A1.

12   *Single Parent Family* magazine, 6/00, p. 5-6.

13   National Fatherhood Initiative, http://www.fatherhood.org/media/consequences-of-father-absence-statistics

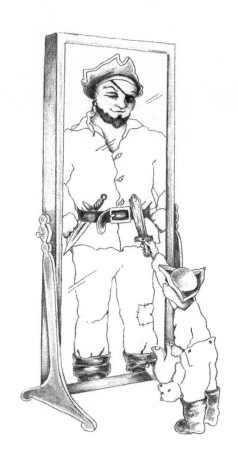

Made in the USA
Charleston, SC
29 December 2016